About Quantum Books

Quantum, the unit of emitted energy. A Quantum Book is a short study distinctive for the author's ability to offer a richness of detail and insight within about one hundred pages of print. Short enough to be read in an evening and significant enough to be a book.

AUTOPSY ON PEOPLE'S WAR

Chalmers Johnson

Autopsy on People's War

University of California Press
Berkeley, Los Angeles, London

University of California Press
Berkeley and Los Angeles, California

University of California Press, Ltd.
London, England

ISBN: 0-520-02516-4 (cloth)
        0-520-02518-0 (paper)
Library of Congress Catalog Card Number: 73-81201

Printed in the United States of America

Contents

Acknowledgments

An earlier version of this essay was presented to the Eighth International Conference on World Politics, sponsored by the Ōa Kyōkai of Tokyo and held at the Hotel Mount Fuji, Lake Yamanaka, Japan, March 26–30, 1973. I should like to express my appreciation to the participants in and sponsors of that gathering for their spirited discussion of people's war and for their autopsy of my autopsy. In addition, Professors Reinhard Bendix, Rupert Emerson, Kenneth Jowitt, Carl Rosberg, Robert Scalapino, Paul Seabury, and Kenneth Waltz took time to read the paper and to offer valuable new ways of looking at the problems involved. None of these people necessarily agrees with the analysis of people's war presented here, and none should be held responsible for the positions I have taken. The subject of this paper is controversial; it is a pleasure to acknowledge the assistance of scholars who have not forgotten the value of scholarly discourse when applied to controversial matters.

1

Introduction

It might be considered bad form, and certainly a matter of
questionable professional ethics, to perform an autopsy on a
body that is not quite dead. Guerrillas and *guérillas man-
quées* around the world, as well as some staff officers of
Western "special warfare" schools, will find it impossible
to agree that an autopsy on people's war is as yet appropri-
ate. My reason for going ahead with the operation anyway
is that, at the present time, we do not really know what we
have on the table in front of us. Was "people's war" ever
alive? Is it dead now, in light of the much acclaimed détente
in east Asia and around the world, and particularly in light
of the withdrawal of American ground forces from Vietnam
and the demise, both politically and literally, of the former
Chinese minister of defense Lin Piao? Is the global spread
of terrorism—the massacre of twenty-six innocent bystanders at Tel Aviv airport during May, 1972; the killing of
Israeli athletes at the Munich Olympics during the summer of 1972; urban guerrilla warfare continuing in Northern Ireland, Argentina, and elsewhere; airline hijackings
occurring during 1972 on an international average of one
every five days; the United States proposal to the 1972
United Nations General Assembly of a draft convention on

terrorism and its subsequent rejection by the General Assembly—a symptom of the health or of the disease of people's war?[1] If China is the great champion of "wars of national liberation," why is it that most of the communist support, other than rhetorical, for recent ones (Bangla Desh, Ulster, even the Palestine Liberation Organization) seems to come from the Soviet Union? These and other questions indicate the need to take stock of as many aspects as possible of the now famous revolutionary strategy known as "people's war," and this requires an exploratory operation that I would be the first to acknowledge might be premature.

Whether this study proves to be an autopsy or a vivisection, the events of 1972 and 1973 clearly marked the end of an era of international involvement in other people's revolutionary struggles. Whatever the future may hold in the way of resorts to political violence, mid-1973 afforded an entr'acte during which we could look back upon and try to assess the extraordinary decade through which we (some of us) had just lived. On January 27, 1973, the four parties involved in the Vietnam war—North Vietnam, South Vietnam, the Vietcong's Provisional Revolutionary Government, and the United States—signed in Paris five documents (an agreement and four protocols) intended to produce a cease-fire throughout Vietnam and to inaugurate peace negotiations among the belligerents. On February 21 a similar agreement for Laos was signed in Vientiane. Need-

[1] Between 1948 and 1958 there were 21 successful cases of aircraft hijacking, an average of 2.1 per year. During the next five years the rate rose to 3.3 per year. During 1969–1970, the average was 50.5 per year, or one every seven days. During 1972 the rate of one every five days was attained. Cf. D. V. Segre and J. H. Adler, "The Ecology of Terrorism," *Encounter* 40, no. 2 (February 1973): 17. For the text of the American draft convention on terrorism of September 25, 1972, see *Survival* 15, no. 1 (January–February 1973): 32–34.

less to recall, the immediate results were disappointing. Hanoi retained at least 145,000 troops in South Vietnam, in accordance with the agreement, and about 70,000 in Laos and 28,000 in Cambodia, in violation of the agreement (chapter 7 of the Paris agreement of 1973 obligates the signatories to respect the 1954 and 1962 Geneva agreements on Cambodia and Laos respectively, including the withdrawal of troops). Fighting, of course, continued throughout Indochina. Nonetheless, on March 29, 1973, the last of what had once been an American expeditionary force of over a half-million men left South Vietnam. The Vietnam war had not ended, but the employment of American ground forces as counterinsurgents in a people's war on the Asian mainland clearly had.

The United States was not the only international actor to change its former policies. During 1972 and 1973 China too offered the revolutionaries of the world a good deal of bitter food for thought, even though it all came tidily packaged in the latest manifestations of Maoist ideology. Even if he ignored China's reversal of the Cultural Revolution, the exchange of quasi ambassadors with the United States, and the overnight discovery that Japanese "militarism" was not reviving after all, a Third World follower of Mao's could not help but observe a few contradictions closer to home.

For example, China sacrificed its former support of the Eritrean Liberation Front in return for Ethiopian recognition of Peking, the establishment of direct flights between China and Africa by Ethiopian Airlines, and a visit by Haile Selassie. Presumably the emperor of Abyssinia had become a member of the "people," and the previously favored Eritreans had ceased to be so. Similarly, the visit of President Mobutu of Zaire to Peking in January 1973 (following Zaire's recognition of the People's Republic in November

1972) must have caused some Africans to recall the years of Chinese attacks on Mobutu and their support with arms and propaganda of the Congolese rebel, Pierre Mulele. Upon his return to Kinshasa, President Mobutu revealed that Chairman Mao had admitted to having lost "a lot of money" in trying to overthrow him, and Mobutu said that he had accepted an interest-free Chinese loan worth $100 million as a recompense for China's earlier assistance to the Congolese rebellion. Whatever else Mao Tse-tung's unusual candor might signify, China by 1973 had changed its foreign policy as fundamentally as had the United States. Even the Soviet Union in the early 1970s seemed at least as interested in trade, détente, and arms control as in supporting revolutionaries in Latin America or Africa. A new guerrilla insurgency will almost surely develop somewhere in the world in the future, but people's war as it was understood in the sixties had died by the early seventies—and that is the occasion for our autopsy.

People's wars, if they are not mere terrorist attacks or commando raids, are a species of revolution, and a note on the author's understanding of "revolution," as used in this book, seems mandatory by way of introduction. Ever since the nineteenth century it has been traditional in Western scholarly analyses of revolution to conceive of the actual outbreak of revolutionary violence as a "dependent variable," that is, as a symptom, or a tragic manifestation, of an allegedly more basic economic or social disorder; and the most profound writing on revolution has sought to uncover and explain these socioeconomic "roots of revolution," be they economic exploitation, class antagonism, racism, backwardness, colonial dependency, and so forth. This approach, of course, reflects the influence of Marx and of the intellectual self-consciousness about revolution that followed the French Revolution. In the wake of the upheavals at the end of the eighteenth century, Western man sought either to incorporate revolution into his philosophies of history (in which revolution became an inevitable "stage" in the history of human "progress") or to reject it on grounds that the social changes seemingly associated with revolution could be attained by an enlightened people without resorting to revolutionary violence. As Jacques Ellul observes, "Until 1789, revolutions were attempted and occasionally achieved, but never romanticized. Then the era of the revolutionary epic began. . . . Revolution literally changed character in the nineteenth century. . . . Revolutionaries [became] more or less convinced that they were moving in the direction of history, that the essential thing was first to identify the direction in order to take it (success depended on it), and that through revolution they were creating history."[2]

This general "reductionist" approach to revolution—that is, the reducing, or rooting, of revolution in the society, or in the economy, or in "history"—lives on today in the pervasive beliefs in both communist and noncommunist countries that revolutions occur because some government, or group, or class, or race is blocking a needed and probably desirable change in social organization. Put crudely, we tend to work on the assumption that there is no such thing as bad peoples, only bad governments; and the very occurrence of revolutionary violence establishes a prima facie judgment in our minds in favor of the rebels and against the authorities.

I do not intend here to dispute the logic or validity of

---

[2] Jacques Ellul, *Autopsy of Revolution* (New York: Knopf, 1971), pp. 86, 117, 118. This book is a translation of Ellul's *Autopsie de la Révolution* (Paris: Calmann-Lévy, 1969).

reductionist analyses of revolution; my own previous work
on the general phenomenon of revolution is squarely in the
reductionist tradition.[3] In dealing with the kinds of revolutionary problems that are discussed in this book, however,
it is necesary to suggest why they stand outside the main-
stream of scholarly studies of revolution. Why, for instance,
are we concerned here with the relationship between the
Chinese doctrine of people's war and the revolutions of the
1960s rather than with discovering the social forces that
have disequilibrated particular social systems and that have
caused particular men and women at particular times to
prefer civil war to social peace?

The topics of our concern here include the pervasive influence of one revolution—the Chinese—on other revolutions; attempts by several nations to "export" or, in Jack
Davis's terms, to "artificially inseminate" revolution;[4] the
effect on any particular (and perhaps genuine) revolutionary
struggle of being drawn into one or the other of the international networks of arms supply, economic aid, sanctuary,
diplomatic recognition, guerrilla training, propaganda support, and so forth; and the problems of theory, doctrine,
plan, strategy, and tactics that preoccupy all actual and as-
piring revolutionary movements today. To quote Ellul
again, and to hint at why traditional theories of revolution
may be inadequate to explain topics such as these, "Revolutions directed toward history are revolutions of theory and
tactics. . . . Because revolutionary spontaneity is rejected,
the 'revolutionary plan' assumes added importance."[5]

[3] Chalmers Johnson, *Revolutionary Change* (Boston: Little,
Brown, 1966).

[4] Jack Davis, "Political Violence in Latin America," International
Institute for Strategic Studies, London, *Adelphi Papers*, no. 85 (February 1972), p. 18.

[5] Ellul, *Autopsy*, pp. 131–132.

It is relatively simple to reconcile an interest in these kinds of topics with the general reductionist, socioeconomic approach to the overall subject of revolution. At the same time, the study of revolutionary doctrine and strategy, of international patron-client relationships on both the revolutionary and counterrevolutionary sides, and of terrorist activities aimed at mobilizing otherwise indifferent populations for revolutionary activities suggest that older theories of a people's "grievances" may actually be misleading when used to explain many of the most important contemporary cases of "revolution."

Take, for example, the problem of the "export" of revolution. Reductionist theory leads to the conclusion that the export of revolution is impossible: because revolution signifies a crisis within a single social system, even if the source of the society's misery comes from the outside (as in the case of imperialism), the crisis cannot be carried across national borders. Even contemporary exporters of both revolution and counterrevolution profess to agree that local governments and peoples must make their own revolution or make themselves immune to revolution through "reform." Regardless of what they professed, however, the world of the 1960s saw a flourishing commerce in the export of revolution and counterrevolution; and from the standpoint of scholarship, the possible futility of this commerce is immaterial. What is interesting and what needs to be studied is the *attempt* to export revolution, the *attempt* to interfere with that export, and the *belief* that both are possible.

In the following pages we shall meet with rather few "rebels," though with quite a few "professional revolutionaries." The distinction is critical. As Ellul puts it, "In comparison with the fashionable modern doctrines of revolution, the efficient apparatus of Leninists and of others, the rebel resembles a poor clod who refuses the history he has already endured and can plainly foresee, which is in store for him, clear as the light of day, tomorrow, as certain as the rising sun."[6] Rebellion is not the same thing as revolution, but it is an intrinsic part of any genuine revolution. Rebellion is the violent, spontaneous act of "ordinary people" saying no! to conditions as they are; revolution is the act of rebuilding the society shattered by rebellion in accordance with a plan or vision (an "ideology") of a more nearly perfect, or equitable, or at least tolerable society. Professionalized revolution is conceivable; professionalized rebellion is not. No doubt there are rebels in the world today and rebellions brewing, but they are as despised by professional revolutionaries as they are by the most reactionary authorities. In fact, rebellion today occurs perhaps more commonly in societies ruled by professional revolutionaries than in any other. In the most general sense, revolution is a saying of both no and yes to history, a combination of rebellion and reconstruction. Where the strings, the puppetry, the propaganda, and the "organization" are all too obviously showing, the analyst should not abandon the socioeconomic concept of revolution, but he should use it very cautiously.

For these reasons, questions about the *need* for revolution in many or most nations around the world are not discussed here. On this occasion I am agnostic on whether the Third World or anywhere else needs more or less liberation, land reform, "green revolution," birth control, employment, ecological protection, dignity, or any of the other aspirations that are commonly supposed to lead to revolutionary activity. I am instead concerned with one particular

[6] Ibid., p. 8.

strategy for making a revolution whether it is needed or not—namely, people's war—and with the campaigns in the 1960s both to sell and to deny this strategy to the majority of the world's self-indentified "revolutionaries."

I propose to conduct this autopsy in the following six discrete stages: (1) historical and ideological origins of the Chinese doctrine of people's war; (2) the high tide of the doctrine during the 1960s; (3) the Vietnam war and its significance for the doctrine; (4) the Soviets' attack on the doctrine, yet their support of people's war; (5) contemporary inconsistencies in the Chinese position; and (6) spinoffs from the doctrine: the myth of the guerrilla.

2

Origins of the Chinese Doctrine
of People's War

Following the Bolshevik Revolution the most important
form of communist theorizing about the further spread of
communism by means of revolution concentrated on the
problem of the "war of national liberation." More significant, all successes actually achieved by communist parties
in coming to power through revolution (as distinct from
being installed by the Red Army)—in China, Yugoslavia,
Vietnam, and Cuba—were based on national liberation
struggles. In terms of revolutionary strategy, communism
has succeeded only when it has been able to co-opt a national liberation struggle, and it has failed whenever it was
opposed to or isolated from a national liberation struggle,
such as those in Israel, Algeria, Indonesia, and Burma.
Needless to add, even when supporting a war of national liberation, the communists have occasionally been defeated,
as in Greece, Malaya, the Philippines, and Venezuela.

Given the failure of internal social revolutions to materi-
alize in the wake of the Bolshevik Revolution, Lenin became the most important communist to perceive that the
lure of "self-determination" for colonized peoples, or other
internationally or ethnically dependent groups, provided

the only basis for authentic revolutionary situations. During the 1920s Lenin adapted Marxist doctrine to these colonial issues, in his formulation of the two-stage (bourgeois nationalist, followed by socialist) revolution occurring in the colonial periphery of "imperialism." Concerning these early days, Isaiah Berlin writes,

> Lenin looked on the Russian Revolution as the breaking of the weakest link in the capitalist chain, whose value consisted in precipitating the world revolution, since, as Marx and Engels were convinced, communism in one country could not survive. Events decreed otherwise, but the doctrine itself was altered only under Stalin. The initial mood among the early Bolsheviks was genuinely antinationalist: so much so that Bolshevik critics in Russia vied with each other in disparaging the glories of their own national literature—Pushkin, for example—in order to express their contempt for national tradition as a central bourgeois value. . . . But after this, the genuine internationalist phase was over. Every revolution and upheaval thereafter contained a nationalist component.[1]

From Lenin's decision to enlist the Communist International in the struggle for national liberation, there developed the characteristic pattern (China, Cuba) of a communist party coming to power through a program of national liberation, anti-imperialism, antifascism, or anti-neocolonialism, and then launching a "dictatorship of development" (Richard Lowenthal's term), justified in the name of an advance toward socialism and communism. This aspect of Leninism also gave rise to the tortuous communist efforts to explain how nationalists and communists are politically compatible with each other and to the endless rationalizations concerning "peaceful transition," "sep-

[1] Isaiah Berlin, "The Bent Twig, A Note on Nationalism," *Foreign Affairs* 51, no. 1 (October 1972): 21.

arate roads," and socialism allegedly growing out of nationalism in the various communist-dominated nation-states. Ho Chi Minh offers an example of the genre: "It is necessary closely to combine patriotism with proletarian internationalism both in the national liberation and the socialist revolution. In the present epoch the national liberation revolution constitutes an inseparable component of the world proletarian revolution, and the national liberation revolution can be crowned with complete success only if it develops into a socialist revolution."[2] J. B. Bell is, however, closer to the immediate point: "When used . . . as something more than a handy cachet, nationalism is by far the most effective basis for revolutionary war. The world-wide vision remains: the vanguard of the vitalized masses fighting wars of national liberation against bestial imperialists; no matter if the masses won't mobilize, the nation is invisible, and the imperialists are local liberals."[3] In short, the primary political tactic of communist revolutionaries since the time of Lenin has been the attempt to forge a "united front" with genuine nationalist movements, thereby hoping to gain mass support for a communist organization not on the basis of the organization's communist values and goals but on the basis of its tactically adopted nationalist values and goals. These facts about the relationships between communism and nationalism that developed after the Bolshevik Revolution and that continue to preoccupy communist theorists to the present day are well known and do not require further synopsis here.[4]

[2] *Pravda*, October 28, 1967.

[3] J. Bowyer Bell, *The Myth of the Guerrilla, Revolutionary Theory and Malpractice* (New York: Knopf, 1971), p. 98.

[4] On the Soviet side, see Adam B. Ulam, *Expansion and Coexistence, The History of Soviet Foreign Policy 1917–1967* (New York: Praeger, 1968), pp. 122–125. For the application of united front

What does require clarification is that the Chinese doctrine of "people's war" arose from the historical communist effort to make the desire for self-determination part of communism's appeal (much in the same way that contemporary Christianity often tries to make socialism part of *its* appeal). During the 1930s and 1940s Mao Tse-tung was a follower of Lenin's, working within the international tradition of communist revolutionary theorizing bequeathed by Lenin. Far from breaking with Lenin, he merely made certain modifications in the overall Leninist "united front" strategy designed to make the strategy work in China. Mao was "creatively applying Marxism-Leninism to the concrete conditions of the Chinese revolution." From these modifications, however, plus thirty years of further observation of wars of national liberation and the development of the Sino-Soviet conflict, there emerged during the 1960s the Chinese doctrine of "people's war."[5]

Mao made three changes. First, he elevated the struggle against imperialism in the colonial periphery to a level of historical significance in its own right, and not simply a blow struck at the European imperialist powers through the "weakest link" in the system. Lenin and later Stalin supported wars of national liberation primarily because they contributed to the possibility of Marxist-type revolutions in mature capitalist states (or to the defense of the Soviet

---

tactics in China, see Lyman P. Van Slyke, *Enemies and Friends, The United Front in Chinese Communist History* (Stanford, Calif.: Stanford University Press, 1967).

[5] See, in particular, John J. Taylor, "The Maoist Revolutionary Model in Asia," *Current Scene* 9, no. 3 (March 7, 1971): 1–19; and Chalmers Johnson, "Chinese Communist Leadership and Mass Response," in Ping-ti Ho and Tang Tsou, eds., *China in Crisis* (Chicago: University of Chicago Press, 1968), 1: 397–437. For the basic Maoist texts, see *Mao Tse-tung on Revolution and War*, M. Rejai, ed. (Garden City, N.Y.: Doubleday, 1969).

Union from attack by such states, e.g., the antifascist alliance after 1935), whereas Mao thought that the Chinese revolution deserved to be prosecuted regardless of international communist priorities or any incidental damage its success might do to capitalist structures in Europe, North America, or Japan.

Second, and following from the first, Mao was never willing after the communist debacle of 1927, when Chiang Kaishek decimated the party, to subordinate the interests of the national communist party to the demands of the nationalist movement. He unquestionably favored a national united front with noncommunist nationalist groups, but he always insisted that the party build its own army and keep that army exclusively under party control. Stalin was quite willing to subordinate local communist parties to the success of a global, Russian-directed antifascist or antiimperialist united front, just as his successors found it much easier than Mao to align themselves with states such as India or Egypt, even though such states might suppress local communists.

Third, and in turn growing from the second point, Mao's retention of a communist military force gave rise to his support for peasant mobilization. By putting the requirements of the Chinese revolution first and having been taught by Chiang Kai-shek's extermination campaigns against the communists that "political power grows out of the barrel of a gun," Mao was inevitably drawn to the necessity of revolutionary armed struggle and to the fact that guerrilla warfare requires a mobilized and sustaining population behind the guerrilla activists. The population of China, like that of most colonized territories, is preponderantly peasant. It is both unnecessary and erroneous to suggest that Mao turned the communist party into a "peasant party." He merely carried the logic of the nationalist struggle to its full implications—namely, to the nationalistic mobilization of *all* the people in the colonized or victimized country.[6]

From these seemingly minor modifications in Leninist thinking, no one of which seems anything more than realistic or a prudent learning from experience, Mao's theory of "people's war," with its emphases on a global countryside in the Third World, a nationalistically aroused peasantry as a leading force, and armed struggle, slowly developed. The essence of "people's war" is that the communists, in the guise of anti-imperialists, should promote the mobilization and organization of peasants in lands subject to imperialist interference, leading to guerrilla warfare and finally to regular warfare against the forces of imperialism and their local allies. It is tactically permissible, according to the doctrine, to enter a united front with a noncommunist nationalist organization in order to promote the struggle and to help legitimize the party as a nationalist force, but the final intention of the effort is to defeat both the imperialists and the other indigenous nationalists, who will by stages be characterized as imperialist "lackeys" (i.e., as traitors).

In mobilizing the peasantry for purposes of supporting guerrilla warfare, purely peasant interests, such as land reform, may be catered to, but it is recognized that the ultimate source and only truly effective basis of peasant mobi-

[6] For an interesting discussion by a Japanese scholar of the distinctive characteristics of Mao's theory of people's war and its relationship to Leninism, see Niijima Atsuyoshi (Waseda University), *Atarashiki kakumei* (New Revolutions) (Tokyo: Keisō Shobō, 1969), pp. 218–243. Niijima writes from a pro-Maoist point of view.

lization will be imperialist depredations, usually as a result of foreign military intervention in order to suppress the burgeoning anti-imperialist movement.[7] As Mao remarked to Edgar Snow in 1965 about the role of imperialism in his own revolution (Snow was required to paraphrase Mao's replies to his questions, hence the use of the third person):

> After reaching an agreement with Chiang Kai-shek to wage a joint war, in 1937, Mao's troops had avoided combat with the main enemy forces and concentrated on establishing guerrilla bases among the peasants. The Japanese had been of great help. They had physically occupied and burned villages over large parts of eastern China. They educated the people and quickened their political consciousness. They created conditions which made it possible for Communist-led guerrillas to increase their troops and expand their territory. Today when Japanese came to see Mao, and apologized, he thanked them for their help.[8]

Shortly after coming to power in 1949 the Chinese communists recognized that these methods of Mao's, which had worked so well for them, were perhaps of broader relevance than just to the Chinese revolution; Liu Shao-ch'i's statement to this effect is well known.[9] However, it was not merely the fact of the communist victory in China, nor even

[7] On land reform and its history in communist revolutionary strategy, see Paul S. Taylor, "Communist Strategy and Tactics of Employing Peasant Dissatisfaction over Conditions of Land Tenure for Revolutionary Ends in Vietnam" (A study for the Foreign Operations and Government Information Subcommittee), House of Representatives, Committee on Government Operations, 91st Congress, 2nd Session (Washington: Government Printing Office, 1970).

[8] Interview with Mao Tse-tung, January 9, 1965, in Edgar Snow, *The Long Revolution* (New York: Random House, 1972), pp. 198–199.

[9] Speech at Trade Union Conference of Asian and Australasian Countries, November 16, 1949 (New China News Agency, Peking, November 23, 1949).

the peasant-based guerrilla wars in Yugoslavia, Indochina, Algeria, and elsewhere, that led the Chinese to hail Mao's doctrines as *the* way to revolution. It was, above all else, the maturing split throughout the 1950s between China and the Soviet Union over correct communist relations with other successful or emergent national liberation movements that produced the Chinese ideology of people's war.

One of the problems with national liberation struggles from a communist point of view is that, as Lenin recognized, they constitute potentially authentic revolutionary situations. In other words, authentic revolutions in the name of self-determination can occur independently of communist influence, authorization, or help. During World War II, for example, the peoples of Indonesia and Burma did not join the international antifascist alliance; instead, they joined the fascists (the Japanese) and gained their independence from European colonialists by way of the Japanese victory. In the Philippines the United States had already sponsored nationalism, thereby making it unavailable for communist exploitation. In much of south Asia, the Middle East, and Africa national liberation was achieved without armed struggle, often without even asking for it, but also without communist leadership.

The Soviet Union and China have a long record of supporting most anti-imperialist movements, but those that succeeded without their sponsorship or assistance have posed a problem for them. In the postwar years up to Stalin's death, both Peking and Moscow were hostile to new "bourgeois nationalist" states; but when various communist operations to subvert them failed, and when the danger arose that they might be organized by the United States into anticommunist alliances, the communist allies began to change their attitude. The Soviet Union at-

tempted to woo the new nations by competing with the
United States in supplying "aid," while China experimented with a low-posture foreign policy known as the
"Bandung spirit." Only in Vietnam did the old Leninist-
Maoist formula still apply, and it built on a World War II
situation similar to that which had prevailed in China and
Yugoslavia. As John Taylor notes, "In Vietnam a unique
situation existed in which local Western colonialists—the
Vichy French—collaborated with the Japanese." [10] Here the
communists had been able to capture the nationalist movement by being both antifascist *and* anticolonialist; but even
here, after 1954, both China and Russia helped put the
revolution on ice for a while as the price of trying to come
to terms with the rest of the Third World.

By the time of the Moscow Conference of 1960, the
Soviet Union had learned how to live with the neutralism
of nations such as India and Egypt—at least they were not
allied with the United States—and the declaration of the
1960 conference accepted the principle that national democratic states could make a "peaceful transition" to socialism. For China, however, despite the relative success of the
Bandung policy from Moscow's point of view, this Russian
willingness to tolerate and even uphold the status quo was
profoundly disquieting. The Russian acceptance of the
situation in the Third World seemed to the Chinese less an
objective appraisal of the situation than an erroneous corol-
lary of Khrushchev's new policy of "peaceful coexistence"
with the United States. The apparent ending of the international communist effort to promote revolution seemed
from China's point of view utterly premature; for one
thing, it left the Chinese unrecognized by the major nations of the world, excluded from the United Nations, and

[10] *Current Scene*, March 7, 1971, p. 7.

surrounded by United States bases from Korea to the Philippines, including Taiwan.

Throughout 1960, following the Moscow Conference, the Chinese harped on the need at least to consider the resort to and support of armed struggle by communist-sponsored movements:

> The working class and the working people, of course, are willing to use peaceful methods to secure state power and transition to socialism. It would be a mistake not to make use of such a possibility if it exists. But the ruling classes will never yield state power of their own accord, and will invariably carry out suppression by violence when people rise and start a revolution. Therefore the working class and its political party absolutely cannot base all their work solely on the possibility of peaceful transition but must prepare at the same time for two possibilities, namely, the possibility of peaceful transition and the possibility of nonpeaceful transition. It would be utterly wrong if peaceful transition is groundlessly described as the only possibility.[11]

Here was the ideological basis for revolutions in independent, noncommunist, Third World states—say, Burma, India, or Indonesia. In the name of the "people," communist parties in such states were urged to make the transition to socialism through armed revolution.

Similarly, with regard to the issue of peaceful coexistence, the Chinese sought to distinguish it from the need for revolutionary wars. The following statement is from the famous Chinese declaration "Long Live Leninism!" that both Moscow and Peking have credited with being the opening shot in the Sino-Soviet polemics:

[11] "Holding High the Marxist-Leninist Banner of the Moscow Declarations," *Jen-min jih-pao*, June 29, 1960.

Peaceful coexistence of different countries and people's revolutions in various countries are in themselves two different things, not one and the same thing; two different concepts, not one; two different kinds of question, not one and the same kind of question. Peaceful coexistence refers to relations between countries; revolution means the overthrow of the oppressing classes by the oppressed people within each country, while in the case of the colonies and semi-colonies, it is first and foremost a question of overthrowing the alien oppressors, namely the imperialists.[12]

The question of whether the Chinese ever fully appreciated the dangers of thermonuclear war and therefore accepted peaceful coexistence between the nuclear powers is highly controversial. The Soviets have charged that Chinese foreign policy in the 1960s was intended to provoke a nuclear war between the superpowers, a war that Mao believed China could survive.[13] On the other hand, two prominent analysts for the United States government

[12] "Long Live Leninism!" *Hung-ch'i*, April 16, 1960. From text in G. F. Hudson, R. Lowenthal, and R. MacFarquhar, eds., *The Sino-Soviet Dispute* (New York: Praeger, 1961), p. 99.

[13] See, in particular, "Nuclear Fetishism and Nuclear Blackmail Are the Theoretical Basis and Guiding Policy of Modern Revisionism," in *The Polemic on the General Line of the International Communist Movement* (Peking: Foreign Languages Press, 1965), pp. 242–248. Mao is probably right about China's capacity to survive a nuclear attack directed against China's population. In a study of China's susceptibility to nuclear deterrence, a group of Japanese scholars calculated that an attack of one thousand warheads against one thousand Chinese urban targets would destroy only 11 percent of the Chinese population. They therefore concluded that China could not be deterred by a simple, antipopulation nuclear capacity such as Japan could conceivably acquire. This Japanese estimate fits with John Philip Emerson's calculation that in 1957 only 15.39 percent of the Chinese population was urbanized, taking concentrations as low as one thousand persons as urban. See *The City in Communist China*, John W. Lewis, ed. (Stanford, Calif.: Stanford University Press, 1971), p. 188.

have argued that China always saw the wisdom of peaceful
coexistence: in one of Alice Hsieh's earliest studies on Chinese military thinking she came to that conclusion, and almost ten years later, Allen Whiting, a former government
official, reconfirmed it.[14] Whatever the case, the Chinese
did believe that it was necessary to keep up communist
pressure on "imperialism," that is, the United States, and
that in order to do so there were means available short of
general war. When the Soviet Union failed to agree, the
Chinese struck out on their own. By the time of the 1963
Moscow Conference, the Soviets were arguing that it was
not even necessary for a national democratic state under
"the influence of the world socialist system" (i.e., a state
friendly to the Soviet Union) to tolerate or legalize a domestic communist party. The Chinese answer to this was
"people's war," sponsored, endorsed, supported, and ideal-
ized—in short, "exported"—by Peking.

The Soviets of course opposed this Chinese position, but
it is important to remember that the USSR in the sixties did
not abandon the possibility of its supporting a war of national liberation. On the contrary, when a "revolutionary
situation," in the Leninist sense (discussed in chapter 5
below), was declared to exist, the Soviets were quite prepared to provide extensive material, political, and techno-
logical assistance to the communist side. In fact, John
Kennedy returned from his 1961 meeting with Khrushchev
in Vienna thinking that it was the Russians, not the Chinese, who were behind the emerging threat of global,

[14] Cf. Alice Langley Hsieh, *Communist China's Military Doctrine
and Strategy* (Santa Monica: The Rand Corporation, Memorandum
RM-3833-PR, October 1963); and Allen S. Whiting, "The Use of
Force in Foreign Policy by the People's Republic of China," *Annals*
402 (July 1972): 55–66.

linked, anti-American "brushfire wars," a threat that de-
manded that the United States acquire a counterinsurgency
capability. Kennedy said at the time:

> In the 1940's and early fifties, the great danger was from
> Communist armies marching across free borders, which
> we saw in Korea. . . . Now we face a new and different
> threat. We no longer have a nuclear monopoly. Their
> missiles, they believe, will hold off our missiles, and their
> troops can match our troops should we intervene in these
> so-called wars of liberation. Thus, the local conflict they
> support can turn in their favor through guerrillas or in-
> surgents or subversion. . . . It is clear that this struggle in
> this area of the new and poorer nations will be a contin-
> uing crisis of this decade.[15]

In retrospect it is evident that the Russians were not prepared to try to foster national revolutionary situations, although they would support them when they developed.
The Chinese *were* prepared to foster them, despite their
formalistic denials of any intent to "export" revolution.
Ironically, it was neither the Russians nor the Chinese who
actually caused the United States to begin to get into the
business of extinguishing brushfire wars. As Jack Davis
observes:

> Even before the missile crisis, events in Cuba had con-
> tributed to a growing sense of urgency among political
> and military leaders in Washington regarding the need
> for a strategy to protect the world position of the United
> States from the dangers implicit in campaigns of polit-
> ical violence in "developing" countries, and the need for
> tactics to counter the supposed special potency of insur-
> gencies and other forms of "irregular warfare." . . . The
> Cuban phenomenon was . . . one of the many factors

[15] Office of Media Services, Bureau of Public Affairs, U.S. Department of State, "Wars of National Liberation," *Viet-Nam Information Notes*, no. 12 (June 1968), p. 3.

responsible for locking the United States into its prolonged and costly engagement against communist insurgency in South Vietnam.[16]

Before we turn to some of the complexities of China's
implementation of the people's war policy, there is one
other doctrinal matter that had rather far-reaching practical consequences and that illustrates the peculiar multi-
plicity of meanings that the term "people's war" came to
have by the end of the 1960s—namely, the varying nuances
of the concept of the "people" in the doctrine of people's
war. Until the 1960s the Chinese meant by the term "people" primarily the large peasant population of a colonized
territory, but during the sixties the term came to be used to
describe any movement, group, race, or ethnic association
that could be mobilized for guerrilla war and that was *not
organized as a state*. Because the Soviet Union had become
a state-supporting power and tended to ally or cooperate
with formal states such as Egypt, France, and India, the
Chinese tended to applaud and endorse movements that
were opposed to states or that were, like China, outside the
international state structure. These movements were said
to represent the "people," and people's war came to have
the connotation that it was different from state-to-state warfare. This accretion of meaning to the term increased its
practical effectiveness; it made it harder for a counterinsurgent state, such as the United States, to clarify for its
own citizens exactly whom it was fighting when it defended
against a people's war.

Steeped in the legalistic concept that wars are between
states, the American public became confused by its govern-

[16] Jack Davis, "Political Violence in Latin America," International
Institute for Strategic Studies, London, *Adelphi Papers*, no. 85 (February 1972), p. 1.

ment's failure to declare war on North Vietnam and thereby identify the *state* with which the United States was at war. Some American citizens accepted the communist propaganda that the United States was an imperialist aggressor in Vietnam. Similarly, in the United States invasion of Cambodia in 1970, the American public seemed disoriented by Cambodia's formal neutrality. In addition, the freeing of the term "people" from the concept of state as applied to warfare increased the capability of communist propaganda to associate "people's war" with "just war," and the widespread use of the phrase "people's war" coincided with the rise of various ethnic protest movements in the United States, which commonly saw themselves as seeking justice from a state that was separated from the "people." All of these connotations of the term "people" as used by Chinese and other supporters of people's war in the sixties greatly complicated the task of the United States in explaining its policies in Vietnam to its own citizens and to its allies.

Needless to say, the United States refrained from declaring war on North Vietnam in order not to threaten China directly and in order to keep the war relatively confined. Moreover, the lack of such a declaration did not prevent the United States from retaliating directly against North Vietnam, despite Hanoi's consistent denials that any People's Army of Vietnam troops were fighting in Cambodia, Laos, or South Vietnam. By contrast, the Israelis have never allowed the concept of the people to interfere with their identification of a belligerent; whenever attacked by "peoples" (i.e., by Palestinian guerrillas), the Israelis have always retaliated against both the guerrillas and the states that supported and harbored them. In general, the Palestinians' use of the concept of the "people," seeking "justice" rather than "victory," has had less effect on Israeli domestic morale and international support than the use of the same tactic by the North Vietnamese had on American morale and international support.[17]

Interestingly enough, by the beginning of the 1970s the concept of the "people" had begun to lose its earlier nonstate meaning for the Chinese, whereas the Russians were increasingly using it with its earlier Chinese connotations. During 1971–72 the Chinese failed to support the "people" and instead supported the state in what was perhaps the most bona fide national liberation struggle of the entire period—in Bangla Desh—and the Soviets were claiming to support the "people"—not only in Bangla Desh but also in Northern Ireland, although of course omitting to mention that the Catholic supporters of the Irish Republican Army in Ulster are a distinct minority among the population.[18] People's war had come a long way since Mao had practiced it against the Japanese and the Kuomintang.

[17] On this subject but from a point of view highly critical of the United States' failure to declare war on North Vietnam, see C. D. Kernig, "Strategic Aspects of Guerrilla Warfare," in Interdoc Conference, Noordwijk aan Zee, June 11–13, 1971, *Guerrilla Warfare in Asia* (The Hague: International Documentation and Information Centre, 1971), pp. 5–6.

[18] For Soviet views on Northern Ireland, see *Pravda*, March 28 and April 23 and 25, 1972. Chinese coverage has been sparse, but see *Jen-min jih-pao*, February 8, 1972. Although most external support for the I.R.A. has come from the United States, some £30,000 worth of arms bound for Ireland was confiscated at Schiphol Airport, Amsterdam, in October 1971; the arms had come from the Czech government. Some I.R.A. men have received training in Cuba in guerrilla warfare, and there is evidence of contacts between Irish revolutionaries and the Quebec Liberation Front and Al-Fatah in the Middle East. On June 11, 1972, the Libyan president, Colonel Kaddafi, claimed that Libya was supplying arms to the I.R.A. He said, "We consider the struggle in Ireland a national one and we will help the free Irish to free themselves from Britain."

3

The High Tide of the Doctrine During the 1960's

During 1965 and 1966 the Chinese carried on an extensive propaganda campaign to elaborate and publicize their doctrine of people's war. The two main sources are former Minister of Defense Lin Piao's *Long Live the Victory of People's War!* of 1965, and *Quotations from Chairman Mao Tse-tung* (the "little red book") of 1966. These are essentially popular, catechismic expositions of revolutionary ideas, and they both originated with Lin's People's Liberation Army. In addition, in 1967 the Chinese published a special little red book entitled *Chairman Mao Tse-tung on People's War*, which contained short excerpts from both Mao's and Lin's writings. Since the Chinese translated all of these materials into virtually every actively used language in the world and disseminated them widely, there can be no doubt that, whatever the internal Chinese intentions in publishing them, many people read them as an invitation by Mao to the revolutionaries of the world to "start shooting." Here are some examples:

From Chairman Mao: "The seizure of power by armed force, the settlement of the issue by war, is the central task and the highest form of revolution. This Marxist-Leninist principle of revolution holds good universally, for China and all other countries."[1]

From Lin Piao's *Long Live the Victory of People's War!*:

Comrade Mao Tse-tung's theory of and policies for people's war have creatively enriched and developed Marxism-Leninism.

History shows that when confronted by ruthless imperialist aggression, a Communist Party must hold aloft the national banner and, using the weapon of the united front, rally around itself the masses and the patriotic and anti-imperialist people who form more than 90 percent of a country's population.

History shows that within the united front the Communist Party must maintain its ideological, political, and organizational independence, adhere to the principle of independence and initiative, and insist on its leading role.

The special feature of the Chinese revolution was armed revolution against armed counter-revolution. The main form of struggle was war and the main form of organization was the army which was under the absolute leadership of the Chinese Communist Party.

It must be emphasized that Comrade Mao Tse-tung's theory of the establishment of rural revolutionary base areas and the encirclement of the cities from the countryside is of outstanding and universal practical importance for the present revolutionary struggles of all the oppressed nations and peoples, and particularly for the revolutionary struggles of the oppressed nations and peoples in Asia, Africa, and Latin America against imperialism and its lackeys.

In a sense, the contemporary world revolution . . . presents a picture of the encirclement of the cities by the

[1] *Quotations from Chairman Mao Tse-tung* (Peking: Foreign Languages Press, 1966), pp. 61–62.

rural areas. In the final analysis, the whole course of world revolution hinges on the revolutionary struggles of the Asian, African, and Latin American peoples.

The peasants constitute the main force of the national-democratic revolution against the imperialists and their lackeys.

The Chinese revolution has successfully solved the problem of how to link up the national-democratic with the socialist revolution in the colonial and semi-colonial countries.

The contradiction between the revolutionary peoples of Asia, Africa, and Latin America and the imperialists headed by the United States is the principal contradiction in the contemporary world.

Viet Nam is the most convincing current example of a victim of aggression defeating U.S. imperialism by a people's war.

They [the Americans] are deeply worried that their defeat in Viet Nam will lead to a chain reaction. They are expanding the war in an attempt to save themselves from defeat. But the more they expand the war, the greater will be the chain reaction.

The Khrushchev revisionists insist that a nation without nuclear weapons is incapable of defeating an enemy with nuclear weapons, whatever methods of fighting it may adopt.

War can temper the people and push history forward. In this sense, war is a great school.

Our attitude towards imperialist wars of aggression has always been clear-cut. First, we are against them, and secondly, we are not afraid of them. We will destroy whoever attacks us. As for revolutionary wars waged by the oppressed nations and peoples, so far from opposing them, we invariably give them firm support and active aid.[2]

These statements, and others like them, were repeated without interruption by the Chinese propaganda services for about five years. Probably no pronouncements by any other government during the 1960s elicited greater attention around the world from friend and foe alike. In the West political and military analysts published numerous books on the mortal dangers to civilization of "many Vietnams," and no less a strategist than B. H. Liddell Hart wrote, "In the past, guerrilla warfare has been a weapon of the weaker side, and thus primarily defensive, but in the atomic age it may be increasingly developed as a form of aggression suited to exploit a situation of nuclear stalemate."[3] Coral Bell went well beyond Liddell Hart's cautious warning: "Though the weapons of mass destruction grow more and more ferociously efficient, the revolutionary guerrilla armed with nothing more advanced than an old rifle and a nineteenth-century political doctrine has proved the most effective means yet devised for altering the world power-balance."[4] In Washington the Cold War bureau-

[2] Lin Piao, *Long Live the Victory of People's War!* (Peking: Foreign Languages Press, 1965), pp. 3, 18–19, 19, 26, 47–48, 48, 49, 53, 57, 58, 59–60, 62, 63.

[3] In Interdoc Conference, *Guerrilla Warfare in Asia* (The Hague: International Documentation and Information Centre, 1971), p. 2. See also J. L. S. Girling, *People's War* (New York: Praeger, 1969); Geoffrey Fairbairn, *Revolutionary Warfare and Communist Strategy* (London: Faber and Faber, 1968); and Douglas Hyde, *The Roots of Guerrilla Warfare* (London: Bodley Head, 1968).

[4] Coral Bell, "Non-Alignment and the Power Balance," *Survival* 5, no. 6 (November–December 1963): 255; quoted in Kenneth N. Waltz, "International Structure, National Force, and the Balance of World Power," *Journal of International Affairs* 31, no. 2 (Summer 1967):226.

cracy invented "counterinsurgency," and by 1967 the various counterinsurgency committees and task forces had proliferated to such a degree that a senior U.S. official warned against a possible "bureaucratic interest" in the existence of people's war.[5]

On the other hand, apologists for Chinese communism outside China justified Mao's and Lin's position by contending that China had only a regional, defensive foreign policy and by accepting Lin's assertion that the United States was an imperialist aggressor.[6] A few analysts steeped in the art of interpreting hidden meanings in communist writings concluded that Lin Piao's statement was nothing more than an esoteric message to Hanoi informing the Vietnamese that China would not intervene in Vietnam and that the Vietnamese would have to be "self-reliant" in prosecuting their people's war.[7] The reason for all these varied reactions was, of course, the eruption of the war in Vietnam. Lin Piao had identified Vietnam as a test case, and Vo Nguyen Giap himself proclaimed, "South Viet Nam is the example for national liberation movements of

[5] "The Odyssey of Counter-insurgency," speech by Thomas L. Hughes, Director of Intelligence and Research, U.S. Department of State, at the Foreign Service Institute, July 3, 1967. Cf. David S. Sullivan and Martin J. Sattler, eds., *Revolutionary War: Western Response* (New York: Columbia University Press, 1971).

[6] See, e.g., Franklin W. Houn, "Chinese Foreign Policy in Perspective," *Bulletin of the Atomic Scientists*, February 1972, pp. 15ff.

[7] See D. P. Mozingo and T. W. Robinson, *Lin Piao on "People's War:" China Takes a Second Look at Vietnam* (Santa Monica: The Rand Corporation, Memorandum RM–4814–PR, November 1965). My own reading of Lin Piao's section on "self-reliance" (*Long Live the Victory of People's War!*, pp. 37–42) is that it is a refutation of the argument that China emerged from World War II on the side of the victors primarily because of the fighting done by other nations. Moreover, Lin is himself quite candid on the subject of foreign aid: "During the War of Resistance Against Japan, our Party maintained that China should rely mainly on her own strength while at the same time trying to get as much foreign assistance as possible" (p. 38).

our time.... If it proves possible to defeat the 'special war-fare' tested in South Viet Nam by the American imperial-ists, this will mean that it can be defeated everywhere else as well."[8] Curiously enough, among the most concerned and most bitterly critical readers of Mao and Lin Piao were the leaders of the Soviet Union, who were simultaneously supplying Hanoi with much of the military means to wage war in the south.

In the United States academic analysts of the Chinese communist press were noticing that Peking made varying levels of endorsement of people's wars around the world—a direct endorsement by Mao Tse-tung of one that was anti-American, down to a mere mention in the newspapers of one that was only anticolonial, and no mention at all of ones that might embarrass a friend or potential friend of China's (e.g., in Somaliland vis-à-vis France).[9] It appeared that the doctrine of people's war was in fact being used, and bent, to serve concrete Chinese foreign policy interests.

Moving beyond the level of verbal endorsements and propaganda support, Western analysts were having a more difficult time identifying, or even conceptualizing clearly, an unequivocal case of "subversion and guerrilla warfare, transported across international boundaries" (President Johnson's words[10]) by the Chinese, except in Burma, Thai-land, and of course Vietnam. Chinese agents were ex-tremely active in this period throughout the Third World, but their efforts at stirring up revolutions had so little prac-tical effect that it was hard not to suspect the Chinese of

[8] *Nhan Dan* (Hanoi), July 19, 1964.

[9] See Peter Van Ness, *Revolution and Chinese Foreign Policy, Peking's Support for Wars of National Liberation* (Berkeley and Los Angeles: University of California Press, 1971), pp. 94–96.

[10] President L. B. Johnson, June 30, 1966, in U.S. Department of State, *Viet-Nam Information Notes*, no. 12 (June 1968), p. 5.

bluffing. In Africa, for example, on July 22, 1965, the Kenya government expelled NCNA representative Wang Te-ming on twenty-four-hours notice, his presence in Kenya being described as "contrary to national security." Similarly, on February 3, 1965, another "NCNA correspondent," Kao Liang, who six years later was a member of the Chinese delegation to the United Nations, was expelled from Burundi together with the entire Chinese embassy staff, for helping rebels in the Congo (Leopoldville), for arming Tutsi refugees from Rwanda in the hope of undermining the Rwanda administration, and for trying to overthrow the Burundi government. In April 1965, Ahmadou Diop, who had attempted to assassinate President Hamani Diori of Niger, confessed that he had received training in China. It was also found that the Chinese had trained and provided the bulk of the equipment for most of the members of the exiled procommunist Swaba party, which had unsuccessfully invaded Niger in October 1964. Such instances of Chinese interference in African and other Third World countries could be repeated at great length. However, in every case, the Chinese were unsuccessful, and their clumsy propaganda tended to alienate the governments concerned. Still, these activities could not be ignored, since the Chinese had succeeded in exporting revolutions to Burma and Thailand during the decade, even though as border and near-border states their cases might not be reliable guides to Chinese policies or capabilities in other continents.[11]

Further complicating the picture was a remark made by

[11] The Burmese and Thai cases are taken up later in this chapter and in chapter 6. NCNA is an abbreviation for New China News Agency, the organization most commonly selected as a cover by Chinese agents engaged in clandestine activities. On Chinese attempts to promote revolution in independent African countries, see Bruce D.

Mao to Edgar Snow during their 1965 talks: "Whenever a
liberation struggle existed, China would publish statements
and call demonstrations to support it. It was precisely that
which vexed the imperialists."[12] This remark suggests the
possibility that Mao and Lin never intended to do much of
anything more to promote people's war other than "publish
statements" and that many people outside of China, not
understanding this (as of course they could not), seriously
overreacted to Chinese bellicosity.

There seem to me to be two ways of looking at this problem of Chinese violent talk and practical nonperformance.
The first might be called the minimalist-maximalist interpretation and the second the internal-external-politics interpretation. In the first interpretation the Chinese ideology
of people's war functioned as a foreign policy tactic for attempting to alter the international status quo, minimally to
cause the United States to cease its support of the Kuomintang on Taiwan, to cause the United Nations to seat China
in the General Assembly and the Security Council (recall
that after Indonesia's withdrawal from the U.N. and prior
to the abortive Indonesian coup of September 30, 1965,
Peking and Jakarta talked of setting up a rival U.N.), and to
cause the advanced industrial nations of the world, including Japan, to recognize the Chinese People's Republic.
Maximally, Peking hoped that its analysis of the world
situation would prove correct, and that with the United
States now cast in the role of Japan in the 1930s, and the
USSR as the equivalent of the Kuomintang, the Chinese

Larkin, *China and Africa, 1949–1970* (Berkeley and Los Angeles:
University of California Press, 1971), pp. 127–132, 179–185.
    [12] *The Long Revolution* (New York: Random House, 1972), p.
217.

communists would emerge as the leaders of a revolutionary world, just as they had emerged as leaders of a revolutionary China twenty years earlier.

If this view is accurate, the maximum advantages that might have been obtained from a global epidemic of people's wars were abandoned by the Chinese fairly early for various reasons. These include the failure of the world communist movement to shift decisively to the support of the Chinese strategy; the alarm and anti-Chinese hostility generated in the Third World (particularly in Africa) by Chinese calls for revolution in countries that were already free of imperialist interference; the increasing threat of a state-to-state war with Russia; the higher risks to China of a people's war escalating into a nuclear war now that China, like the United States and the USSR, had become a nuclear power; and the achievement, according to one interpretation of the Vietnam war, of China's minimal demands as a result of America's "defeat" there. Denis Warner, for example, contends, "The détente with China was the offspring of American disenchantment with Vietnam."[13] So the argument goes that as the conditions of international isolation that China had objected to in 1960 were alleviated and as the menace of a Soviet strike against China's nuclear capacity loomed larger, Mao settled for the minimal gains from his people's war policy and initiated a new, Bandung-like policy of coexistence with the international state structure.

The internal-external-politics interpretation suggests that virtually all of the polemics about people's war were a smoke screen for the Cultural Revolution, which was co-terminous with the campaign to promote people's wars, and

[13] Denis Warner, "The Morning After the War Before," *Atlantic*, December 1972, p. 118.

that the Cultural Revolution itself was basically an internal
struggle between the Communist party leadership and
Mao Tse-tung, who was making a comeback after the loss
of much of his power in the wake of the Great Leap Forward. In this analysis the theory of people's war was mostly
intended to bolster Mao's prestige for internal political
purposes, and what went on outside of China was neither
intended nor even under firm control in Peking. In fact,
most of the antics of Red Guards outside of China, the
urban terrorism carried on by Peking's supporters in Hong
Kong during 1967, and the Chinese attacks on foreigners
who failed to honor Mao's works or portrait all over the
world were so damaging to China's foreign relations that
Mao terminated the Cultural Revolution, at least in part,
in order to correct the situation and to avoid offering the
Soviet Union a temptingly isolated China as a target.[14]

Even the insurgency in Burma, although it had been in
existence for some twenty years, reached an unprecedented
peak of violence in 1967 primarily as a result of the zeal of
functionaries inspired by the Cultural Revolution rather
than because Chinese leaders genuinely believed that a
people's war could succeed there. After the Cultural Revolution was over, Mao received Ne Win in Peking, and the
war subsided to its earlier level of intensity. In Thailand,
one careful study of the people's war there concludes that it
began in the early 1960s as a direct response to the increasing American buildup and that by the end of the decade,
with the American threat declining, the Thai revolutionaries in exile in Peking were spending much more time sing-
ing the praises of Mao Tse-tung than realistically attempt-

[14] For an analysis along these lines, see Philip L. Bridgham, "The
International Impact of Maoist Ideology," in Chalmers Johnson, ed.,
Ideology and Politics in Contemporary China (Seattle: University of
Washington Press, 1973), pp. 326–351.

ing to mobilize the Thai peasantry.[15] It should be noted
that both of these insurgencies continued after the Cultural Revolution was over, but the immediate point is that
both also displayed aberrations—one in terms of increased
violence and the other in terms of decreased violence—
reflecting the influence of the Cultural Revolution (we
shall return to these two cases in chapter 6).

Similarly, in the disputes that divided communist parties
around the world, the pro-Chinese factions devoted more
effort to having Mao recognized as the "greatest Marxist-
Leninist of the present era" than to persuading their parties
to act on Mao's ideas. The dispute with the Soviet Union
was over substantive foreign policy differences, but it also
concerned internal Chinese politics in that Mao's political
enemies were more sympathetic to a renewed Sino-Soviet
relationship than Mao was. Mao's chief enemy in the Cultural Revolution, Liu Shao-ch'i, was of course charged
with being pro-Soviet and was dubbed "China's Khrushchev." On the Russian side, they hoped that Mao's domestic foes would help them solve their "China problem" by
deposing Mao Tse-tung once and for all. Most significantly,
the Chinese used those splinter parties that endorsed Mao's
ideas on people's war to attack the Russians, and not actually to promote people's wars. For example, a recent study
notes:

> The principal focus of Chinese propaganda and activities
> in Latin America during the 1960's was not the "imper-

[15] See Daniel D. Lovelace, *China and "People's War" in Thailand,
1964–1969* (Berkeley: Center for Chinese Studies, University of
California, China Research Monograph no. 8, 1971). On Burma, see
Harold C. Hinton, *China's Turbulent Quest* (Bloomington: Indiana
University Press, 1972), p. 244. Cf. R. A. Scalapino, *Asia and the
Major Powers* (Washington: American Enterprise Institute, 1972),
p. 23.

ialist" foe but the pro-Moscow Communist Parties and the USSR itself for following the "parliamentary road." Although events such as the Panama crisis of 1964 and the Dominican Republic episode of 1965 received heavy propaganda treatment, PRC propagandists devoted far more attention to the pernicious ideological influence of the USSR than to the U.S. role in Latin American affairs.[16]

Clearly the minimalist-maximalist and internal-external interpretations are compatible with each other and should be combined. Mao and his "close comrade in arms Lin Piao" launched the policy of verbal popularization and support of people's war for a variety of concrete Chinese ends. They wished (1) to prevent Russia and the United States from freezing the international status quo on the use of force while China's national needs were unfulfilled; (2) to cause the United States to end its policy of isolating and blockading China; (3) to portray Mao Tse-tung as a great Marxist-Leninist theoretician in order to enhance his domestic political prestige and to weaken the Soviet Union by challenging its right to lead the international communist movement; and (4) to see if a combination of postcolonial discontent in the Third World and major miscalculations by the United States might lead to a situation that China could exploit but that would probably remain subnuclear. In order to obtain these ends, China did not have to do anything more than talk a lot and provide sufficient arms to establish its credibility.

Credibility, of course, rests in the eye of the beholder. An international actor can do various things to increase his credibility, but whether his enemies and those dependent upon him actually believe what he says depends upon cir-

[16] "Peking and Latin America: Rewriting the Scenario," *Current Scene* 9, no. 4 (April 7, 1971): 1.

cumstances that he can only affect, not control. Like the concept of role, credibility is a relational concept, and a nation cannot be credible all by itself. The 1960s odyssey of people's war is relevant to the concept of credibility because China's enemies, the United States and the USSR, believing strongly in the need to counter Peking's pronouncements on revolution, did as much as Peking itself to promote a global belief in either the danger or the advent of people's war. We shall turn to the USSR's contribution in chapter 5; the contribution of the United States was counterinsurgency.

It is hard to believe in retrospect that Peking would have been taken as seriously as it was during the sixties if the United States had not taken people's war so seriously. Given the sharp American reaction to Chinese talk about people's war, it is not surprising that many potential revolutionaries not otherwise likely to have been influenced by China came to the conclusion that guerrilla warfare, or a variant of it, was most likely to bring them success.

In addition to providing credibility for Chinese propaganda, counterinsurgency is important as a direct part of the people's war equation: if counterinsurgency is misconceived or ineptly implemented, it becomes "imperialist aggression," that is, it becomes a part of the problem instead of the solution. Virtually all theories of guerrilla warfare, Mao's included, contend that counterguerrilla measures by the defending power or his patron cannot be effective (despite a good deal of evidence to the contrary), and they hold (or hope) that counterinsurgent operations will merely contribute to a general peasant mobilization. Going even further than theories of guerrilla warfare, all terrorist and urban guerrilla strategies are based on an attempt to *elicit* a counterinsurgent overreaction from the status quo power.

The Brazilian guerrilla leader, Carlos Marighella (who was killed in a police ambush on November 4, 1969), explains why: "It is necesary to turn political crisis into armed conflict by performing violent actions that will force those in power to transform the political situation of the country into a military situation. That will alienate the masses, who, from then on, will revolt against the army and police and blame them for this state of things." [17]

As a matter of fact, terrorism usually leads to a military coup d'etat against the comparatively open government that allowed terrorists to exist. For example, Jack Davis notes that "most of the seventeen successful military coups during the 1960's (affecting ten countries) [in Latin America] were at least in part a reaction to the threat, immediate or imagined, of revolutionary violence." [18] By contrast, there were no successes at all for those who employed revolutionary violence. The masses rarely rise against such military regimes—the chances of success, easily calculated, are minimal—but, of course, in the long run such a right-wing coup might lead to potentially revolutionary conditions as a result of investment funds being transferred to military spending, general economic stagnation in the wake of perpetual political crisis, and so forth. In the meantime, however, the military regime will have killed or imprisoned all actual or potential revolutionaries. Terrorism is oriented toward trying to create revolutionary conditions where none exist; usually the most that it accomplishes is to contribute to the communist ideological prophecy that bourgeois nationalist governments, in Latin America for example, are

[17] Quoted in Robert Moss, *Urban Guerrillas, The New Face of Political Violence* (London: Temple Smith, 1972), p. 13.

[18] Jack Davis, "Political Violence in Latin America," International Institute for Strategic Studies, London, *Adelphi Papers*, no. 85 (February 1972), p. 2.

"military oligarchies," incapable of improving the lives of
the people, by helping to install and perpetuate such military oligarchies.[19] There is, moreover, nothing inevitable
about military regimes being failures at economic development and reform. In Brazil, Peru, and Algeria military
regimes have been fairly effective, and when they do badly,
they still manage to do as well as most civilian regimes.

Mass-based guerrilla warfare and counterinsurgent operations are not the same things as terrorism and military
coups, but they do have something of the same relationship
to each other. Perhaps the major difference is that counterinsurgency has proven rather less obviously effective in
suppressing guerrillas than military oligarchies—for example, the Greek colonels, the Uruguayan army, or the military government of Turkey—have been in suppressing terrorists and urban guerrillas. Counterinsurgency is a delicate
political-military maneuver that is forced to pass between
the Scylla and Charybdis of over- or underreaction and commonly ends up hitting both.

Generally speaking, counterinsurgency operations are
oriented toward separating the active guerrillas from the
mass of peasants who are in various stages of mobilization
and who provide the guerrillas with their military advantage
of superior intelligence, as well as recruits, logistical support, and labor. Counterinsurgency can be undertaken to
win the peasantry away from the guerrillas, or to identify
and attack the guerrillas in order to keep them away from
the peasants, or both. However it is done, it should not contribute to peasant grievances and hence to further peasant
mobilization.

There is an enormous literature, as well as folklore, on

[19] Cf. Alphonse Max, *Guerrillas in Latin America* (The Hague:
International Documentation and Information Centre, 1971).

American counterinsurgency in Vietnam, and although the particular Vietnamese intricacies are not directly relevant to our topic, a few details will illustrate the relationship between people's war and counterinsurgency. Most early approaches to the problem, including this author's,[20] advocated the policy of attracting the peasantry to the defending authority's side, what has unfortunately come to be known as "winning hearts and minds," or in the military argot of Vietnam, WHAMing the peasantry. Foreigners usually do not know what, if anything, will attract the peasantry of a particular country, and theories abound about what exists in the hearts or minds of the Vietnamese peasants. They range from Denis Warner's belief that all Asians are more attracted by "good political ideas" than by "a loaf of bread," to Tanham and Duncanson's contention that "it is the probable, not the desirable, that commands peasant support."[21] In a different context, Duncanson complicates the picture by arguing, "In Malaya we cultivated the people's hearts through their minds, not their minds through their hearts," although he does make the point that the rectitude and political style of a counterinsurgent force are as important as what it does or what it gives.[22] Too often obvious things are forgotten in a counterinsurgency program, such as devising ingenious methods whereby the public can provide information about guerrillas to the authorities without risking their own lives. Counterinsurgents seem unaware of how commonly the police of a defending power are penetrated by the revolutionary party and therefore how dan-

[20] Chalmers Johnson, "Civilian Loyalties and Guerrilla Conflict," *World Politics* 14, no. 4 (July 1962): 646–661.

[21] Warner, in *Atlantic*, December 1972, p. 122; George K. Tanham and Dennis J. Duncanson, "Some Dilemmas of Counterinsurgency," *Foreign Affairs* 48, no. 1 (October 1969): 120.

[22] Interdoc Conference, *Guerrilla Warfare in Asia*, p. 71.

gerous it is to an informant to have his name in a police file.

In one of the most sophisticated studies of counterinsurgency, Nathan Leites and Charles Wolf, Jr., advocate replacing WHAM with a "cost-benefit" model, and although they do not specifically advocate it, a reader less sophisticated than the authors in econometric modeling might get the idea from their work that counterinsurgency is most effective when understood as a process of raising the costs to the peasantry of supporting the guerrillas.[23] Although this seems highly plausible in theory and may well have worked in practice in Vietnam (that issue is discussed in the next chapter), most historical evidence on defeated guerrilla insurrections suggests that raising the costs to the peasantry of supporting the rebellion only spreads and intensifies the rebellion. On the other hand, actions taken to alleviate peasant discontent combined with positive government, effective law enforcement, *and* military action against the insurgents can isolate the activists. Among many historical studies, John Womack's book on Zapata's rebellion in the Mexican Revolution illustrates both the costs of repression and the efficacy of WHAM.[24] By contrast, in a more recent context, Gerald Bender argues that Portuguese counterinsurgency measures, primarily population relocation, have given greater impetus to the people's war in Angola that began in 1961 than anything done by the guerrillas.[25] Perhaps the ultimate approach to this problem has been to try to create a counterguerrilla infrastructure on the side of the defenders that does not depend on peasant support—

[23] Leites and Wolf, *Rebellion and Authority, An Analytic Essay on Insurgent Conflicts* (Chicago: Markham, 1970).

[24] John Womack, Jr., *Zapata and the Mexican Revolution* (New York: Random House, 1968).

[25] Gerald J. Bender, "The Limits of Counterinsurgency: An African Case," *Comparative Politics* 4, no. 4 (April 1972): 331–360.

for example, the IBM-Philco Task Force Alpha, or the "electronic battlefield" that was utilized in Vietnam. Unfortunately, to judge from published accounts, it did not work—the displays either showed too few militarily attractive targets, or the enemy figured out how to decoy the sensors, and the jungle seemed alive.[26]

Turning to the opposite aspect of the issue, direct military operations against the insurgents, Mao Tse-tung is categoric in saying that "our strategy and tactics are based on a people's war; no army opposed to the people can use our strategy and tactics."[27] This may be true, but it does not rule out using nonguerrilla strategies and tactics against guerrillas, even though the costs will be high to the peasantry, and hence to the defenders, in doing so. In a sense this was done in Vietnam, forcing the communist side to alter its strategy and tactics in the direction of conventional warfare and thereby also raising the costs to it in terms of the support it received from the peasantry. Wherever the cost and benefit curves have intersected in Vietnam, it is clear that it has been costly to the peasantry there to support either or neither side.

Interestingly enough, Herbert Marcuse agrees with this analysis and believes that a technologically advanced society can always defeat a people's war. He asserts:

> Any romantic idea of the liberation front is incorrect. Guerrilla struggle as such does not present any mortal threat to the system: in the long run it cannot resist a technological "Final Solution." The system reserves for itself the right to decree whether and when it will achieve "victory" by burning and poisoning everything. . . . This tendency can only be broken if the resistance of the victims of neo-colonialism finds support in the "affluent

[26] *San Francisco Chronicle,* September 16, 1972, p. 10.
[27] *Quotations from Chairman Mao Tse-tung,* p. 98.

society" itself, in the metropolis of advanced capitalism and in the weaker capitalist countries whose independence is threatened by the metropolis.[28]

This argument has of course formed the theoretical rationale during the 1960s for some "student" insurrections and urban guerrilla warfare in advanced industrial nations. We shall return to this form of people's war later, but suffice it for now to note that "counterinsurgency" against this form of insurrection has proved to be comparatively easier and more effective than counterinsurgency against rural guerrillas.

In sum, the 1960s witnessed the high tide of both Chinese sponsorship of people's wars and also of the Western reaction to them. No doubt the latter would not have existed without the former, but there can equally be no doubt that "the men of order by elaborating and extending their response out of proportion to the reality of the threat" contributed greatly to the spread and attractiveness of the original doctrine.[29] This is not to imply that there should have been no response at all to Chinese propaganda. It is clear in retrospect that the Chinese were playing to the hilt the well-known role of the agitator who pushes the frontline strikers forward or who incites a mob to violence. However, the response to this might easily have included a range of activities short of direct military intervention in guerrilla campaigns—for example, greater propaganda support of Khrushchev and an earlier and more vigorous exploitation of the Sino-Soviet dispute, a more careful choice of the

[28] Herbert Marcuse, "On Revolution," in Alexander Cockburn and Robin Blackburn, eds., *Student Power* (Harmondsworth, England: Penguin, 1969), p. 368.
[29] J. Bowyer Bell, *The Myth of the Guerrilla* (New York: Knopf, 1971), p. 258. Cf. George K. Tanham, "Some Insurgency Lessons from Southeast Asia," *Orbis* 16, no. 3 (Fall 1972): 646–659.

places in which to "demonstrate" Western counterinsurgent capabilities (i.e., ones in which the West was most likely to win, rather than places on the Chinese border), and a greater commitment to the training of allied and U.S. counterguerrilla forces ("Green Berets") in order to avoid reliance upon non-specially-trained, conscripted, American combat divisions. Most important, a well-honed response to Chinese policies required careful analysis of the basis of each guerrilla war in order to ensure that American efforts were directed against the "export" of revolution, not the suppression of genuine revolution. In many cases (e.g., Indonesia, discussed in chapter 5), doing nothing was better than overreacting, thereby letting the communist side make the mistakes and allowing the West to exploit the contradictions that all too obviously existed in Chinese people's war doctrine. Finally, if Western political leaders judged that intervention in a dubious case was indispensable—for example, Laos—then it would seem that something like the Central Intelligence Agency's rather desultory and uninspired counterinsurgency there, much derided in the press throughout the period, more accurately fitted the problem than the enormous campaigns against guerrillas mounted elsewhere in Indochina. The Laotian approach did not actually make the situation worse, which was an achievement of sorts.

4

The Vietnam War

Both Lin Piao and Vo Nguyen Giap identified the Vietnam war as a test case for the efficacy of people's war. The United States too saw the war as a test of methods for resisting people's war. Therefore, any study of people's war is obliged to consider Vietnam and try to find out how the test came out. Unfortunately, the results are ambiguous: on one level of analysis the United States and South Vietnam stopped people's war cold, even if at a rather high cost, while on another level of analysis the Vietnam war may have validated a particular theory of people's war. This validation, however, could not have brought much pleasure to Mao Tse-tung since the theory under test was only tangentially related to his. An analysis of the relationship between the Vietnam conflict and people's war is thus of greatest significance in the present context in showing how the concept of people's war has developed and is continuing to be adapted to new political-military circumstances.

The two levels referred to above are, first, people's war considered as a credible military means for employing revolutionary force, the sense in which Mao and Lin Piao have used the term, and second, people's war considered as a "psychomilitary strategy," what Douglas Pike has called "neo-revolutionary guerrilla warfare" and what the present writer has referred to as the "third generation of guerrilla warfare."[1] In the first sense, guerrilla warfare is undertaken as a realistic, judo-like strategy in which an objectively weaker military power turns the tables on a muscle-bound imperialist power and defeats it in a contest of arms—for example, the way the Chinese communists defeated the armies of the Kuomintang and their American backers. The definition of victory here is military victory. In the second sense—which might also be called the Franco-Vietnamese-Algerian tradition of revolutionary war—guerrilla warfare is undertaken not ultimately to obtain a favorable military decision in a "third stage" showdown but rather to unnerve and bring to their knees an imperialist power and its client by shattering their will. Victory here is political. Too often journalistic commentators on wars of national liberation have failed to observe this distinction, one that is frequently made by practitioners of revolutionary war themselves; and they have therefore seriously confused the discussion about who has won or lost what in Vietnam.

In terms of the first sense of guerrilla warfare—the one in which the concepts of peasant mobilization, an anti-imperialist national front, clandestine munitions and possible sanctuary support from allies, and protracted war are central—none of the people's wars of the sixties did very well, including the one in Vietnam. Vo Nguyen Giap himself has admitted a loss of 600,000 men in fighting between

[1] The term "psychomilitary strategy" is used by J. Bowyer Bell, *The Myth of the Guerrilla* (New York: Knopf, 1971), p. 59. Also see Douglas Pike, "Guerrilla Warfare in Vietnam," in Interdoc Conference, *Guerrilla Warfare in Asia* (The Hague: International Documentation and Information Centre, 1971), pp. 48–64; and Chalmers Johnson, "The Third Generation of Guerrilla Warfare," *Asian Survey* 8, no. 6 (June 1968): 435–447.

1965 and 1968, out of a total manpower pool of about 5,000,000, while the Americans put the total number of "communists" killed in Indochina between 1961 and 1972 at 863,577.[2] Moreover, by about 1970 at least 80 percent of the day-to-day combat in South Vietnam was being carried on by regular People's Army of Vietnam (PAVN) troops, perhaps 96,000 of them, rising to 145,000 by the time of the 1973 agreement. Genuine black-pyjama southern guerrillas—that is, the People's Liberation Armed Force of the National Liberation Front—had been decimated and amounted to no more than 20 percent of the communist fighting force.

By 1972, Hammond Rolph concluded, "We are no longer studying a true guerrilla insurgency. A regular professional army of a communist state is operating outside its borders in conventional style against a modernized South Vietnamese Army and the fire-power of the U.S. Air Force." He also added, "Sympathy for the Viet Cong may still be widespread in rural areas today, but its relevance to victory for the party is dubious. Triumph now depends on the military prowess of the North Vietnamese Army, not on the linkage between the party and the rural population."[3] A year earlier Frank Trager wrote, "In purely military terms,

[2] U.S. Department of Defense, Office of the Assistant Secretary of Defense for Public Affairs, *Southeast Asia Casualties Statistical Summary* (Washington: July 27, 1972). United States losses were 45,828 men killed in action out of 2,300,000 who served in Vietnam since 1965. Another 10,065 died in noncombat accidents in the Indochinese theater, and some 303,243 were wounded. As of March 16, 1971, the United States admitted to the loss of 3,248 fixed-wing aircraft and 4,318 helicopters. From 1965 to the end of 1971 the war had cost about US$126 billion. Cf. Milton Leitenberg, "America in Vietnam: Statistics of a War," *Survival* 14, no. 6 (November–December 1972): 268–274.

[3] Hammond Rolph, "Vietnamese Communism and the Protracted War," *Asian Survey* 12, no. 9 (September 1972): 785, 789.

the war in South Vietnam is now on the threshold of victory. . . . That is, the Vietnamese and Allied Forces have defeated the North Vietnamese attempt at a conventional 'third phase' war take-over in South Vietnam."[4]

Virtually all serious specialists on the Vietnam conflict tend to agree with Rolph that the guerrilla infrastructure ceased to be a major factor in Hanoi's revolutionary strategy in about 1969, except for propaganda and legitimizing purposes. However, they also doubt that the final outcome of the Vietnamese civil war will be decided solely by the clash between the PAVN and the "Vietnamized" forces supporting Saigon. In a sense even the PAVN regulars are present in South Vietnam only for propaganda and credibility purposes (and, of course, they are never identified by Hanoi as North Vietnamese troops). For some time communist strategy has rested more on psychological considerations and what Douglas Pike calls the "externalization program" than it has on purely military considerations.

Vietnamese thinking about people's war has diverged from purely Maoist principles at least since the time of the Franco-Viet Minh conflict, a war in which the Viet Minh emphasized international communist support, morale-destroying but militarily indecisive strikes such as Dien Bien Phu, and the mobilization of external sympathy for its cause, in addition to guerrilla warfare. Mao Tse-tung was not insensitive to psychological warfare issues or to an attempt to sap the enemy's will to continue (consider, for example, his policies on the careful treatment of prisoners of war in order to try to weaken the morale of the rank-and-file of the opposing forces), but he never based his strategy on these tactics.

By contrast the Vietnamese have always tended to under-

[4] Interdoc Conference, *Guerrilla Warfare in Asia*, pp. 82–83.

stand military means more in terms of their political shock
effect than in terms of the damage actually inflicted on the
enemy's armies. As a result the Vietnamese communists
never devoted as much attention as Mao did to building up
revolutionary bases founded squarely on peasant mobilization and organization, even though they did much of this
prior to 1965.[5] Of course, they were not as dependent on
peasant support as Mao was; the Vietnamese revolution has
always received external support from the Soviet Union and
China undreamed of by the Chinese communists during or
after World War II. In a sense, Ho Chi Minh and Vo
Nguyen Giap merely built upon Mao's strategy by adding
to it themes peculiar to their own tradition—particularly
the tradition of Dien Bien Phu, that is, the attempt to so
bloody the enemy in a single stroke that his political supe-
riors lose their will to continue. Tet of 1968 and the offensive of 1972, both undertaken in years of American pres-
idential elections, were in the Dien Bien Phu tradition, and
were intended to produce the same spectacular results in
Washington that the 1954 battle produced in Paris.

Mao and other Chinese strategists have often been critical of the Vietnamese willingness to launch "decisive battles" that are of dubious military significance and that
always damage the support and legitimacy that the communists can expect to receive from the people of the target
area.[6] Nevertheless, the Vietnamese can point to some ex-

[5] Cf. Jeffrey Race, *War Comes to Long An, Revolutionary Conflict in a Vietnamese Province* (Berkeley and Los Angeles: University
of California Press, 1972), particularly chap. 4.

[6] See Brian Shaw, "China and North Vietnam: Two Revolutionary
Paths," parts 1 and 2, *Current Scene* 9, nos. 11 and 12 (November
and December, 1971): 1–12, 1–12; and King C. Chen, "Hanoi vs.
Peking: Policies and Relations—A Survey," *Asian Survey* 12, no. 9
(September 1972): 806–817.

ternal confirmation of their approach. Whereas Peking has rarely talked about the strategic significance of the Algerian revolutionary war, a communist spokesman and former guerrilla in the Philippines, William J. Pomeroy, writes in a Soviet-authorized publication, "The Algerian liberation war . . . never had to develop from guerrilla to regular war to win; the French army was not defeated militarily, the political victory being greatly advanced by mass demonstrations in cities and by the political crisis in France provoked by the protracted and costly imperialist wars first in Indochina and then in Algeria."[7] Tet-like offensives might weaken the support and legitimacy the communists could obtain from the peasants of South Vietnam, but Hanoi believed that such offensives could increase the support and legitimacy the communist side received from citizens and opposition politicians in North America and Western Europe.

Even though the Vietnamese have long experimented with shortcuts in Mao's "protracted war," Douglas Pike dates Hanoi's decisive shift to psychomilitary operations from 1969. He believes that Vo Nguyen Giap and Le Duan committed themselves to this strategy after they assessed the failure between 1965 and 1969 of more-or-less regular revolutionary guerrilla warfare. This failure was due to the overwhelming mass and movement of United States forces.[8] If Pike's analysis is accurate, what evaluation should we make of the effectiveness of this variant theory of people's war? Clearly, it is too soon to come to any final conclusions. Denis Warner, however, believes that Hanoi has been successful. He writes,

[7] William J. Pomeroy, ed., *Guerrilla Warfare and Marxism* (New York: International Publishers, 1968), p. 37.
[8] In Interdoc Conference, *Guerrilla Warfare in Asia*.

The Tet offensive [of 1968], though a costly military failure for Hanoi, had been Washington's psychological Dien Bien Phu. Everything that happened thereafter, the declaration of personal surrender by President Johnson, the protracted halt in the bombing, the Paris talks, the Guam Doctrine, Vietnamization, and all the rest, represented a signal lowering of American sights, the abandonment of American hopes of winning a military victory in Indochina and of reinstating unhappy South Vietnam as a "pearl in the crown of the free world," to borrow one of the lyrical descriptions of the official American propagandists in the late 1950s.[9]

Historians may well accept this judgment. Certainly the Vietnamese revolution going back to 1945 has had as great an impact on the development of people's war as the Chinese or Algerian revolutions. It put the final stamp of approval on guerrilla warfare as the central theoretical focus of *all* contemporary strategic thinking about revolution, and it eclipsed once and for all the older Bolshevik orientation toward organization of workers, revolutionary situations, and "ten days that shook the world." As J. B. Bell remarks, "After Dien Bien Phu the guerrilla-revolution became the way of the future par excellence."[10] Moreover, in its more

[9] *Atlantic*, December 1972, pp. 117–118. It is perhaps worth noting that "the declaration of personal surrender by President Johnson" might well be taken as evidence for the opposite of Warner's point of view. As Kenneth Waltz observes, "The Korean case is one in which the President and his closest advisers had failed to sustain the nation's confidence in their integrity and competence. Under such circumstances, if a change of persons and parties can be easily and gracefully made, policies that remain necessary though they have become unpopular can more easily be continued. The election of 1952, by bringing a change in government, promoted the continuity and success of a policy. This is hardly what is wanted by the critics of America's policy in Vietnam." "The Politics of Peace," *International Studies Quarterly* 11, no. 3 (September 1967): 209. Although President Johnson's political demise could hardly have been called "graceful," it certainly had the effect that Waltz predicted in 1967.
[10] *The Myth of the Guerrilla*, p. 36.

recent manifestations, the Vietnamese example contributed greatly to the divergence between older, Maoist ideas of guerrilla warfare as a technique of military attrition and the newer ideas of Guevara, Fanon, Debray, and Marcuse, who separate guerrilla activities from mass support, purely military goals, party supervision, or even (in the case of Fanon) from political objectives (we shall return to these trends in a later chapter). The Vietnam war opened in a radically new way the question of what precisely constitutes "victory" in a revolutionary war and gave rise to this rule of thumb: "If the defenders don't win, they lose; if the guerrillas don't lose, they win."

5

The Soviet Union and People's War

Even a cursory reading of any of the large number of recent Soviet books on Maoism and the Chinese theory of
revolution leaves no doubt about the accuracy of Klaus
Mehnert's conclusion: none of this work "shows any evidence of serious and worthwhile research on Maoism by
Soviet experts," and "the reader who might expect to obtain important information about the last few decades of
China's history from Maoism's most intimate enemies finds
himself disappointed."[1] Instead, one confronts a barrage of
epithets, including "petty-bourgeois revolutionism," "anarchism," "Trotskyism," "hurrah revolutionism," and "bar-
racks communism."

This body of work is important, however, for three reasons: (1) by its very vehemence and widespread distribu-
tion among leftist groups, it has contributed to the credibility of people's war (idealism about the Soviet Union, like
that about the United States, is at a low ebb around the
world, including some of the USSR's client states; when
the Soviets attack Mao, as well as Fanon, Debray, and

[1] Klaus Mehnert, "Mao and Maoism: Some Soviet Views," *Current Scene* 8, no. 15 (September 1, 1970): 8 and 9. This article con-
tains an extensive bibliography of Soviet writings on contemporary
China.

others, many people cannot help but believe that the object of attack must be important and efficacious); (2) it offers a form of Marxist-Leninist explanation for the failures of people's wars during the 1960s, and thereby invites some disappointed communist followers of the guerrilla road to turn to the Soviets for leadership and at the same time disguises the extent to which the Soviet Union, like China, supports only those revolutions that serve Soviet state interests; and (3) the apparent reasonableness and high-minded responsibility displayed by Soviet writers over issues such as the possible escalation of a revolution into global war obscures the extent to which the Soviet Union has actually been arming some selected revolutionary groups around the world.

The Soviet dissection of Mao's strategy of revolution begins with the proposition "There are not and cannot be universal forms of struggle suitable in all conditions."[2] The Chinese are said not to understand this principle. Instead, the Chinese believe that any form of struggle other than revolutionary war—including parliamentary contests, co-operation with non- or presocialist movements or states, and workers' movements in advanced capitalist societies—are bourgeois deceptions designed to deflect or co-opt a revolution. Indeed, in "Long Live Leninism," the Chinese asserted that "revolution means the use of revolutionary violence by the oppressed class, it means revolutionary war," a quotation that Russian writers like to hurl back at the Chinese.[3] In addition to this erroneous reliance on only one form of struggle, the Chinese are also said to have narrow-

[2] Boris Leibson, *Petty-Bourgeois Revolutionism* (Moscow: Progress Publishers, 1970), p. 73.

[3] Text in G. F. Hudson, R. Lowenthal, and R. MacFarquhar, eds., *The Sino-Soviet Dispute* (New York: Praeger, 1961), p. 101. Cited by Leibson, p. 71.

mindedly concluded that peasants alone can be a significant
revolutionary force, that the national liberation struggle is
the most important force directed against imperialism, and
that the former colonial Third World is revolutionary while
the advanced, urbanized world is not. All of this contributes, in Soviet eyes, to the splitting of the world revolutionary front and to the advance of imperialism. "If all the units
of the world revolutionary movement," writes N. Simoniya,
"would start emphasizing their own merits and arguing
about their contribution to the common struggle, they
would achieve nothing except disunity and would become
sidetracked from the revolutionary struggle under way."[4]

In answer to these one-sided Chinese propositions, the
Soviets hold up the traditions of Lenin's great flexibility and
his "correctness." The element that contemporary Soviet
writers most repeatedly cite from Lenin's large corpus of
writings on revolution is his definition of the "revolutionary
situation." According to Y. Krasin, "A people's revolution is
inevitably preceded by a revolutionary situation. It was
Lenin who developed the concept 'revolutionary situation'
and discovered the laws governing its rise and development."[5] What, then, is a revolutionary situation? In " 'Left-
wing' Communism, An Infantile Disorder" (1920) Lenin
argued, "The fundamental law of revolution, which has
been confirmed by all revolutions, and particularly by all
three Russian revolutions in the twentieth century, is as follows: it is not enough for revolution that the exploited and
oppressed masses should understand the impossibility of
living in the old way and demand changes; it is essential for
revolution that the exploiters should not be able to live and

[4] N. Simoniya, *Peking and the National Liberation Struggle* (Moscow: Novosti Press Agency Publishing House, 1970), p. 9.
[5] Y. Krasin, *Lenin, Revolution, and the World Today* (Moscow:
Progress Publishers, 1971), p. 106.

rule in the old way. Only when the '*lower classes*' *do not want* the old way, and when the 'upper classes' *cannot carry on in the old way*—only then can revolution triumph."[6]

This definition furnishes Soviet writers with several advantages: they are able to declare when and where a genuine revolutionary situation exists in accordance with whatever interests they wish to serve, and in the case of a miscall they can fall back on the tautology that because an insurrection failed, no "revolutionary situation" existed. Actually, Mao has no difficulty in agreeing with Lenin here, although Mao's strategy is oriented toward making it impossible for the upper classes to carry on in the old way, whereas Lenin believed that a "political crisis," only partly engineered by the communists, would be required to dissolve the rulers' capacity to govern and suppress rebellion. Where Mao and Lenin differ is on the question of what the lower classes want. Mao asserts dogmatically that "the people of all countries, the masses comprising more than 90 per cent of the entire population, sooner or later want revolution," whereas Lenin keeps that question open: "We cannot tell, and no one can tell beforehand, how soon a real proletarian revolution will flare up . . . and *what immediate cause* will most serve to rouse, kindle, and impel into the struggle the very wide masses who are presently dormant."[7] Given this situation, Lenin advocates that "in order to fulfill its task, the revolutionary class must be able to master *all* forms, or aspects, of social activity without any exception . . . [and] the revolutionary class must be ready to pass from one form

[6] V. I. Lenin, *"Left-Wing" Communism, An Infantile Disorder* (Moscow: Foreign Languages Publishing House, n.d.), p. 81. Italics in original.

[7] Premier Chou En-lai repeated this famous statement of Mao's to Edgar Snow in 1970, *The Long Revolution* (New York: Random House, 1972), p. 162. For Lenin, see *"Left-Wing" Communism*, p. 95 (italics in original).

to another in the quickest and most unexpected manner."[8]

During the 1960s, it would seem, the Soviets did have a somewhat better average than the Chinese in picking revolutionary situations in which to intervene. The Soviets can claim to have identified Bangla Desh, anti-Zionism in the Middle East, Cuba, and perhaps Northern Ireland, while also paying the bills in Vietnam; whereas China's record is Vietnam, perhaps half a dozen barely simmering insurgencies in progress (Burma, Thailand, Malaysia, the Philippines, Sarawak, and Mozambique), and opposition to Bangla Desh.

The Leninist definition of a revolutionary situation seems accurate enough, leaving aside all questions of the inevitability of such situations arising and of the role of classes in them, but it is at too high a level of generalization necessarily to exclude Mao's understanding of revolution. Nevertheless, and without belaboring the issue, Soviet writers would seem to be correct in arguing that Mao and particularly Lin Piao have been extremely, and perhaps fatally, narrow in advocating guerrilla warfare in support of Third World wars of national liberation as the only kind of revolution in which a contemporary communist ought to get involved. Soviet critics of Mao are quite able to incorporate guerrilla tactics into the repertoire of a "correct" communist, but they always make the appropriateness of their use dependent upon the revolutionary situation. Thus, for example, Krasin writes:

> The armed action of vanguard detachments can hasten the development of the revolutionary situation and the outbreak of the revolution only when the symptoms of the revolutionary situation have already appeared in

[8] *"Left-Wing" Communism*, p. 94.

political life and when there is a growth among the people of revolutionary sentiments which ensure their sympathy and support of the armed vanguard and are a source of fuel for the fires kindled by the sparks of armed struggle. . . . Some active proponents of guerrilla warfare claim that there is no need to wait for objective conditions for revolution.[9]

In a somewhat more charitable version of the same argument, Pomeroy observes,

In all countries with deep-seated social wrongs there are apt to be, at any given time, some people who can be inspired to take to arms, even when a revolutionary situation does not obtain, in the hope of changing their conditions of life. Such acts, whether spontaneous or conspiratorially planned, are viewed by Marxist-Leninists as isolated cases of desperation or adventurism, and as symptoms, not as solutions, of social problems.[10]

Having concluded that the Chinese leaders really do not know what they are talking about when it comes to revolution, Soviet critics then turn to the question that really interests them: Why should the Maoists think the way they do? This question is important in Moscow because, of course, the disagreement over people's war is not only, or even primarily, an argument about tactics. The Russians are not just trying to set their Chinese colleagues straight on how to make a revolution. They are instead using the case of people's war to illustrate the totally degenerate and renegade quality of Mao's communism. In order to do that the Soviets must pin on Mao the labels of the Marxist-Leninist sins: anarchism, adventurism, extreme "Left" (al-

[9] *Lenin, Revolution, and the World Today*, p. 120.
[10] William J. Pomeroy, ed., *Guerrilla Warfare and Marxism* (New York: International Publishers, 1968), p. 10.

ways in quotes) opportunism, and Trotskyism. Since these terms do not describe objectively verifiable traits or attitudes and are, in fact, entirely matters of ideological definition, the Russians' task is rather simple.

Krasin offers one of the higher-quality Marxist explanations for the appearance in China of "petty bourgeois" tendencies. He traces the origins of these deviations to China's comparatively backward levels of socioeconomic development and dates their appearance from the Great Leap Forward in 1958. In his view, the Leap manifested petty-bourgeois revolutionism on the domestic front, while the campaign to promote people's wars, which followed the Leap in the sixties, marked its eruption in the realm of foreign policy. Krasin's argument is worth quoting:

> Low levels of economic and social development confront proletarian or revolutionary-democratic parties coming to power as a result of socialist or national-democratic revolutions with extremely difficult problems. And the situation is complicated by the fact that the social environment, since it is not adequately suited to the fulfillment of the tasks facing these parties, inevitably tells in one way or another on their own policy and conduct. Petty-bourgeois mentality and the powerful bourgeois tendencies linked with it create the tempting illusion that it is easy to resolve economic difficulties and to advance rapidly along the socialist or non-capitalist path by political means alone. This illusion finds expression in the bombastic slogan that "politics is the commanding force." . . . New forms of social organization are implemented by decree and are not reinforced by appropriate deep-going socio-economic reforms. Instead of being based on real economic possibilities, they are based on speculative schemes. Hence, the typically petty-bourgeois illusion that ideal revolutionaries can appear in any economic condition and that, relying solely on their

consciousness, they can build new ideal forms of social life in the face of all opposition and despite all material obstacles.[11]

Petty-bourgeois revolutionism having appeared in China, the more serious affliction of Trotskyism could not be far behind. And, indeed, "The main thing in Trotskyism is its endeavor to jump at any cost over stages of revolutionary development. . . . Mao Tse-tung holds the same methodological views as the Trotskyists as regards both the subjectivist striving to jump over stages and the contraposing of the revolution in one country to the world revolution."[12] It is doubtful that arguments of this kind actually do much damage to the integrity of China's proposals even among Marxist-Leninist groups, particularly since the audience addressed today is more concerned with whether the proposals work than with Trotsky's alleged espousal of them. Concretely, Mao's theory of revolution is to the left of Lenin's and in the direction of Trotsky's. Whatever the Chinese may have intended by their calls for people's war, they have excited the interest and approval of groups around the world that call themselves Trotskyist.[13] There

[11] *Lenin, Revolution, and the World Today*, pp. 65–66.

[12] Leibson, *Petty-Bourgeois Revolutionism*, p. 68.

[13] Ibid., p. 105. Although Trotskyism as a doctrinal alternative to Stalinism seems to have little relevance to the world of the sixties and seventies, Trotskyist groups continue to exist and are often characterized by greater flexibility and openness to new trends and tactics than orthodox, Moscow-oriented groups. With regard to the United States, for example, Brian Crozier observes: "Three main tendencies were apparent in the old revolutionary Left—Maoist, Stalinist, and Trotskyist. The Trotskyist Socialist Workers' Party and its youth affiliate, the Young Socialist Alliance, remained firmly in control of the main antiwar organizations, the National Peace Action Coalition and the Student Mobilization Committee to End the War in Vietnam. They not only organized demonstrations against American policy in Vietnam but also began to focus attention on other areas such as the Middle East." *Annual of Power and Conflict, 1971*, Brian Crozier, ed. (London: Institute for the Study of Conflict, 1972), p. 26.

have been some cases of unification between self-designated
Maoists and self-designated Trotskyists for joint revolutionary action—for example, in Japan, where the Sekigun-ha
(Red Army Faction), which is avowedly Trotskyist, joined
with the Keihin Ampō Kyōtō (Tokyo-Yokohama Joint
Struggle Group Against the Japan-U.S. Security Treaty),
which is avowedly Maoist, to become the Rengō Sekigun
(United Red Army), the organization that on May 30,
1972, carried out the terrorist killing of twenty-six persons at
Lod Airport, Tel Aviv.[14] Maoism is not Trotskyism, but
groups outside of China inspired by Mao's writings (and
sometimes praised in the Chinese press) have found that
they have affinities with Trotskyists.

In addition to attaching old Marxist-Leninist labels to
the Chinese, the Russians also charge that Maoist policies
lead to disaster—and these are the more important charges.
The Soviets cite two important cases, in addition to numerous smaller ones. The first is Indonesia. According to
Soviet writers, the Chinese are responsible for the communist catastrophe that occurred in Indonesia on September
30, 1965. The Communist party of Indonesia (PKI), in
league with various sympathizers in the armed forces, attempted to carry out a coup by killing the top military
leaders of the country. Although the communists did kill
some generals, the army itself rallied, turned on the party
as well as Chinese and Chinese-affiliated persons in the
country, and exterminated them. It is interesting that the

---

[14] See Yoshihiro Kuriyama, "Terrorism at Tel Aviv International
Airport and a 'New Left' Group in Japan," *Asian Survey* 13, no. 3
(March 1973): 336–346; "Sekai kakumei sensen wa koko made kite-
iru" (The World Revolutionary Front Up to Date), *Shūkan yomiuri*,
August 5, 1972, pp. 16–21; and Shisō Undō Kenkyū-jo (Institute for
the Study of Ideological Movements), ed., *Sayoku hyaku shūdan*
(One Hundred Leftist Groups) (Tokyo: Zenbō Sha, 1972), pp. 360
et seq.

Soviets blame the Chinese for this purge of communists, since it could easily be argued that the PKI's tactics were closer to Lenin's than to Mao's. However, the Soviets charge that Maoist propaganda misled D. N. Aidit, the party leader, into believing that a revolutionary situation existed in Indonesia, that Indonesia's ties to the Third World were more important than its ties to the USSR, and that a "Peking-to-Jakarta" axis could be the spearhead of socialism in Asia.[15]

Many Western specialists on Indonesia doubt that the Chinese communists had any direct involvement in the coup at all—other than perhaps suggesting it and encouraging the PKI to undertake it, just as in the following year (1966) Mao explicitly urged visiting Japanese communist leaders to launch guerrilla warfare in Japan, something that the Japanese communists wisely refused to do and that led to an open breach between the Japanese and Chinese communist parties.[16] Whether under Chinese control or not, Aidit had for some years prior to 1965 spoken in a primarily Chinese vocabulary, thereby possibly alarming the Indonesian military. It is conceivable that the coup of September 30 was only a desperate communist attempt to head off a military coup against them. Whatever the actual case, it

[15] Simoniya, *Peking and the National Liberation Struggle*, pp. 16–19.

[16] Note the conclusions of Kyosuke Hirotsu: "At the heart of the [CCP-JCP split] is Peking's insistence that Chairman Mao's strategy of 'people's war' and violent revolution apply to all countries, including a modernized, economically advanced nation such as Japan. . . . The JCP leaders, however, saw the unsuccessful 1965 'September 30' coup attempt in Indonesia, backed by the Indonesian Communist Party (PKI), as an effort by PKI leader Aidit to carry out the Chinese plan. The utter failure of the attempt is believed to have finally convinced [JCP secretary-general] Miyamoto and other JCP leaders to discard Peking's policies." "Trouble Between Comrades: The Japanese Communist Party's Turn Away from Peking," *Current Scene* 5, no. 4 (March 15, 1967): 1, 4.

is significant that Lin Piao's idea of the world's countryside surrounding the cities was propounded by D. N. Aidit almost two years before Lin paid him the compliment of incorporating it into *Long Live the Victory of People's War!* In December 1963, Aidit told a plenum of the Indonesian Communist Party's Central Committee:

> On a world scale, Asia, Africa, and Latin America are the village of the world, while Europe and North America are the town of the world. If the world revolution is to be victorious, there is no other way than for the world proletariat to give prominence to the revolutions in Asia, Africa, and Latin America, that is to say, the revolutions in the village of the world. In order to win the world revolution the world proletariat must go to these three continents.[17]

The Soviets regard such statements as nationalistic bombast, typical of China's contribution to the world communist movement. They argue that the disaster of 1965 not only demonstrated the error of such thinking but also compounded the problem by bringing to power an anticommunist regime in a country that the Soviet Union had tried to cultivate with several billion dollars worth of aid.

Until the autumn of 1965 both the United States and the USSR had some reason to fear that the Chinese could bring all of southeast Asia under the Peking-Jakarta axis. Sukarno's confrontation with Malaysia and the Vietnam war were closing the pincers on Thailand and Malaysia. However, when the Indonesian pole fell away and the United States intervened in Vietnam, the focus of the Soviet Union's fears changed, and it decided to come to North Vietnam's aid, supplying most of its military material and,

[17] D. N. Aidit, *Set Afire the Banteng Spirit! Ever Forward, No Retreat!* (Peking: Foreign Languages Press, 1964), cited in "A Plea for People's War," *Current Scene* 3, no. 28 (October 1, 1965): 1.

above all, providing the modern weapons required to fight the United States.

The Soviets imply that they have always been firm supporters of the Vietnamese communists, but they also cite the Vietnam war as another concrete instance in which Chinese thinking has led the world communist movement astray. The Soviets contend that Mao's refusal to agree to a joint action with them in support of Hanoi prolonged the war and, in fact, allowed the United States to intervene without risking thermonuclear war with Russia. "Many people realize now," writes Boris Leibson,

> that the U.S.A. would never have dared to escalate the war in Vietnam had it not been for China's stand. There is a direct connection between the escalation of the war in Vietnam and the fact that, while the Mao Tse-tung group confines itself to threats as far as U.S. imperialism is concerned, it actually opposes the Soviet Union, obstructs it and other socialist countries in their assistance to Vietnam, and endeavors in every possible way to prolong the conflict, hoping that it will grow into a world war.[18]

The Chinese of course respond that it was only Chinese pressure that caused the Soviet Union to pay any attention at all to Vietnam. As for the charge that China tried to promote the Vietnam conflict into a world war, Mao Tse-tung told Edgar Snow that he feared that Russia was trying to involve China in a war with the United States over Vietnam, as the Soviet Union had done once before in Korea.[19]

These charges and countercharges by both sides in the Sino-Soviet dispute cannot, of course, be settled in favor of one or the other. They merely illustrate the extent to which both China and the Soviet Union have shaped their "theo-

[18] *Petty-Bourgeois Revolutionism*, p. 107.
[19] *The Long Revolution*, pp. 19–20.

ries" of revolution to suit their national policies. At the same time, they cannot readily disown the theories should the policies prove unsuccessful, since to do so would be to abandon one's identity as a communist and to hand over the legacy of Marxism-Leninism to the other side. Which is to say that in this age of political sociology, when so much political behavior and most political ideologies are reduced by analysts to other factors such as self-interest, culture, or personality, ideas still continue to generate political action, even if the motives for living up to the ideas are sometimes more complex than the ideas themselves.

6

China and People's War After the Cultural Revolution

In his report to the Ninth Congress of the Chinese Communist party held in April 1969, Lin Piao described the objectives of China's foreign policy as follows: "To develop relations of friendship, mutual assistance and cooperation with socialist countries on the principle of proletarian internationalism; to support and assist the revolutionary struggles of all oppressed people and nations; to work for peaceful coexistence with countries of different social systems on the basis of the five principles; . . . and to oppose the imperialist policies of aggression and war." There happens to be what the Maoists would call a "contradiction" in this statement. Number three of the five principles of peaceful coexistence mentioned by Lin is "mutual noninterference in each other's internal affairs"; but by any standards (including those of China itself, which holds Tibet and Taiwan to be internal affairs), foreign support for and assistance to an internal revolutionary struggle constitutes "interference" in the domestic affairs of a "different social system." How the Chinese have dealt with this contradiction following the Ninth Congress may offer some clues to future developments in China's support of people's wars.

Perhaps the first point to make is that while support for some people's wars by a foreign power may constitute interference, it apparently is a practice quite acceptable to an overwhelming majority of the members of the United Nations. During the autumn of 1972 the U.N. General Assembly voted 99 to 5 to recognize the "legitimacy of anticolonial armed struggle."[1] Although General Assembly resolutions do not have the effect of creating international law, they point in that direction; and this resolution therefore raises real doubts about the continued "illegality," according to international law, of foreign aid to revolutionaries. China and the USSR were among those voting for the resolution, while the United States, Portugal, South Africa, Great Britain, and France were opposed. Needless to say, this U.N. resolution was aimed primarily at Portugal, South Africa, and Rhodesia. According to the reports of U.N. committees, there are still some thirty million people living under colonial rule, concentrated primarily in Angola, Mozambique, Portuguese Guinea, Rhodesia, South Africa, and Southwest Africa (known at the United Nations as Namibia).

The 1972 General Assembly session also welcomed Amilcar Cabral, the Marxist-Leninist secretary general of the Partido Africano da Independência da Guiné e Cabo Verde (PAIGC), who became the first leader of a liberation army to be accorded observer status by the United Nations. (It was, unfortunately for Cabral, a short-lived status: on January 20, 1973, at his place of exile in Conakry, Guinea, Cabral was assassinated, probably by one of his own followers in the PAIGC, which has been torn by dissension be-

[1] *New York Times*, November 5, 1972.

tween Africans and Cape Verdeans.) A similar degree of official United Nations recognition was also accorded to the Mozambique Liberation Front (Frelimo, or Frente de Libertaçaô de Moçambique). These matters are relevant here because China is continuing to provide active support, including the supply of arms and the training of guerrillas in bordering Tanzania, to the insurgency in Mozambique.[2] However, given the fact that the United Nations accords special status to wars of national liberation in Africa, and the fact that all of the African revolutionary organizations are special targets of Sino-Soviet competition, Mozambique and other insurgencies in southern Africa probably should be regarded as long-term commitments rather than as important bellwethers in Chinese policy.

Another special case that should probably not be used as a guide to China's future policies is the situation in the Middle East. China has expressed strong support for the Palestinian guerrillas ever since the Arab-Israeli conflict of 1967. Following the defeat of the armies of the Soviet-supported Arab states, China quickly championed the non-state-affiliated guerrillas who went into action in the wake of the defeat. There has long been a mission in Peking of the Palestine Liberation Organization (PLO), and on April 14, 1972, *Jen-min jih-pao* endorsed the PLO's activities as follows: "The Chinese government and people always support the just struggle of the Palestinian and other Arab peoples. We are convinced that the fighting Palestinian people, persisting in revolutionary unity and protracted armed struggle and maintaining vigilance against all enemy

[2] "Africa's Mini-Vietnam," *Newsweek*, November 27, 1972, pp. 46–48. The best analysis of all aspects of the various southern African liberation movements is Sheridan Johns, "Obstacles to Guerrilla Warfare—A South African Case Study," *Journal of Modern African Studies* 11, no. 2 (1973): 1–37.

schemes, will undoubtedly overcome temporary difficulties on their road of advance and will win final victory in their struggle."

Despite numerous statements such as this during 1972 and several receptions of PLO representatives by Chou Enlai, it would appear that Chinese influence among the Middle Eastern guerrillas is declining. At the Arab People's Conference for the Support of the Palestinian Revolution, which met in Beirut during the last week of November 1972, the Soviet-allied Arab states and representatives of the communist parties of the USSR, Hungary, Poland, East Germany, Bulgaria, Rumania, and Yugoslavia set up a new front to support the Palestinian guerrillas. (Also present at the conference were representatives of the Vietnamese NLF and the Uruguayan Tupamaros.) The conference clashed over Yassir Arafat's demand that the guerrillas' backers reject outright the U.N. Security Council's resolution calling for a peaceful settlement of the Arab-Israeli conflict, but it finally compromised with a decision to reject all "submissive solutions" to the Middle East situation.[3] Thus, even though the guerrillas' orientation would seem to be closer to Peking's than to Moscow's, it appears likely that the Soviet Union, because of its considerably greater ability to deliver on promises of arms, has beaten back China's challenge to its position in this area.[4]

[3] *New York Times*, December 3, 1972.

[4] One exception to this general Middle Eastern picture is the insurgency in the independent sultanate of Oman. Led by the Popular Front for the Liberation of the Occupied Arabian Gulf and active in Dhofar province since 1963, the "Dhofar war" began as a nationalist struggle but was taken over in 1967 by Maoists, some of whom had reportedly been trained in China. PFLOAG receives material support from abroad via the People's Democratic Republic of Yemen— that is, the former British colony of Aden—and in January 1973 Omani authorities claimed to have recovered large caches of Chinese-marked arms in the course of attacks on the insurgents. The war in

Elsewhere China's own foreign policy has changed radically since the height of the campaign to promote world revolution in the mid-sixties. Having obtained a large measure of international recognition from the United Nations and most of the nations of the world, and having seen the Sino-Soviet dispute turn toward direct national confrontation, China's foreign policy is starting to resemble that of the Soviet Union a decade ago. In 1970 Chinese offers of credit to developing nations approached $700 million, making China the leading donor of economic assistance among communist nations during that year; and China is by far the biggest source of communist aid to Tanzania and Zambia. In addition, the Chinese have begun to voice approval of the nonaligned policies of many Third World countries, including, in 1971, praise for Sierra Leone and Algeria. In the statements on the establishment of diplomatic relations with Equatorial Guinea (October 15, 1970), Ethiopia (November 24, 1970), and Nigeria (February 10, 1971), the Chinese specifically referred to the five principles of peaceful coexistence as the basis for friendly relations. All of these signs of moderation of course led up to, and conditioned, the détente with the United States and the exchange of ambassadors with Japan.[5]

Verbal support for people's wars has declined over the past few years. The January 1, 1972, joint editorial of *Jen-*

Dhofar consumes a large percentage of the Oman budget each year, and the insurgents appear to be well established. It is of course possible, even likely, that the Soviet Union will attempt to gain control of this revolution, given its strong geopolitical interests in the area. On the Oman war, see *Annual of Power and Conflict, 1971*, Brian Crozier, ed. (London: Institute for the Study of Conflict, 1972), pp. 48–49; *Current Scene* 10, no. 12 (December 1972): 8; and *New York Times*, January 14, 1973, and April 15, 1973.

[5] See the symposium, "China's New Diplomacy," *Problems of Communism* 20, no. 6 (November–December 1971): 1–32.

min jih-pao (People's Daily), *Hung-ch'i* (Red Flag), and
Chieh-fang-chün pao (Liberation Army News), which is an
annual survey of national policy, made only two references
to it: "Local wars between aggression and resistance to aggression and between revolution and counter-revolution
have never ceased," and "From the strategic rear areas of
imperialism to the 'heartland' of capitalism, revolutionary
struggles are surging forward." The January 1, 1973, editorial continued this trend, replacing the usual references to
people's war with emphasis on China's efforts to forge a
united front with the Third World against superpower
"hegemonism" and power politics.

It appears that China is haltingly abandoning its former
commitment to subversion and revolution in the Third
World, and accepting the need to work with the uncom-
mitted, noncommunist nations as they actually exist there.
China's outspoken opposition to the influence of the big
powers in the United Nations, its support of the particular
nationalistic causes of nations such as Chile, Peru, and
Panama, and its approval of the plan to make Latin America a nuclear-free zone are all signs of this new policy. China
still believes that the world balance-of-power can be altered
by organizing the Third World as a bloc, but it is going
about trying to do this organizing in a more pragmatic and
less dogmatically revolutionary manner.

It is of course possible that what looks like a trend may
only be temporary. For example, W. A. C. Adie notes that
China's support for the Tanzam railway project may have
revolutionary as well as economic objectives: "Apart from
. . . altering the East African center of gravity away from
Nairobi to the more radical Dar es Salaam, and orienting
Zambia northwards instead of southwards, one Chinese

idea behind the railway has been to overcome Zambia's dependence on railways through white-controlled territories, so as to enable its ideal geographical situation as a guerrilla base to be fully developed." These potentialities do exist, but the previous record of China's influence in Africa suggests that it could not promote a guerrilla struggle from Zambia that did not also have the support of African leaders. As for Chinese aid, Adie comments, "The African leaders seem confident that they will be able to do a Sadat on the Chinese when the time comes."[6]

China has not ceased altogether advocating people's wars. Particularly with regard to revolutionary movements in southeast Asia, there has been only a gradual diminution of rhetorical support; and on May 19, 1971, the first anniversary of Mao's statement of May 20, 1970, expressing continued support for the communist war effort in Indochina, all the Peking newspapers carried a long article on communist progress in Burma, Thailand, the Philippines, Malaysia, and North Borneo. More than a year later, on July 21, 1972, *Peking Review* published an Asian "Armed Struggle Roundup," which reported on action in South Vietnam, Laos, Thailand, Malaysia, and Palestine (now included as part of Asia), but which ignored Burma and the Philippines.[7] This continuing interest in people's war in Asia has led some commentators to speculate that China may be

[6] The reference of course is to Egyptian President Sadat's 1972 expulsion of Russian advisers from Egypt after receiving large quantities of aid from the Soviet Union. See W. A. C. Adie, "China's African Wedge," *To the Point* (South Africa), November 18, 1972, pp. 18–19; and Adie, "China Returns to Africa," *Current Scene* 10, no. 8 (August 1972): 1–12.
[7] Cf. Deirdre M. Ryan, "The Decline of the 'Armed Struggle' Tactic in Chinese Foreign Policy," *Current Scene* 10, no. 12 (December 1972): 7.

carrying on a "two-tiered" policy of blending "people's war" and "people's diplomacy."[8] As we shall see subsequently, the evidence on this point is contradictory, but the trend appears to be toward a decline in Peking's support for wars of national liberation, both those on other continents and those close to home.

One of the interesting questions about this change in China's emphasis on people's war is whether it has anything to do with the death and denunciation of Lin Piao. According to internal party documents that became available outside of China in the summer of 1972, Lin Piao, who was last seen in public on June 3, 1971, was ousted as minister of defense and is now dead because he plotted an armed uprising against Mao Tse-tung in an attempt to establish army rather than party supremacy within China. Some Chinese leaders have stated explicitly that the crisis surrounding Lin arose because of his personal ambition after becoming Mao's heir apparent at the 1969 party congress, and did not involve ideological controversy.

Nonetheless, the Chinese press has been creating an ideological basis for Lin's differences with Mao in order to explain Lin's ouster to the public (as in the case of Liu Shao-ch'i during the Cultural Revolution, Lin and his supporters were not mentioned by name during 1972 but only referred to as "swindlers like Liu Shao-ch'i"). Lin Piao's ideological vilification has also involved the usual rewriting of history—for example, the 1948 Liaohsi-Shenyang campaign is now said to have been under the personal control of Mao, who allegedly had to countermand disastrous orders of Lin's in order to win it. As a matter of fact, Lin Piao was

[8] "Revolutionary Rhetoric and People's Diplomacy," *Current Scene* 9, no. 8 (August 7, 1971): 9–10; and Interdoc Conference, *Guerrilla Warfare in Asia* (The Hague: International Documentation and Information Centre, 1971), p. 86.

the field commander in this campaign, and Mao was elsewhere at the time.[9]

With regard to Lin's written works, in late October 1970 copies of the *Quotations from Chairman Mao Tse-tung* (the "little red book"), which Lin had edited, were withdrawn, and a new volume of the "five most important philosophical works" of Mao replaced them. On February 14, 1972, a new edition of Mao's quotations went on sale in Peking in English, Spanish, Korean, and Vietnamese, but not in Chinese. Except for a few alterations in the translations, the only difference was the deletion of the preface by Lin Piao on how best to study Mao's works. This incident suggests that Mao did not object to the Little Red Book but only to Lin's former use of it to promote the People's Liberation Army and the cult of personality. Lin Piao's *Long Live the Victory of People's War!* is no longer available in China in Chinese, but it has not been specifically denounced in the press. Even if it were, this would not necessarily constitute a change in regime policy, since Lin has been downgraded for political, not ideological, reasons. If the regime disagreed with the general principles contained in *Long Live the Victory of People's War!* it would surely have attacked that work first of all, since it is by far the most important thing Lin Piao ever wrote. Therefore, it seems that whatever may happen to *Long Live the Victory of People's War!* neither its lack of circulation nor the entire Lin Piao affair reveals anything about trends in China's policies toward people's wars.

The real test of whether China will continue to try to export revolution is to be found not in what China says but

---

[9] For the revised history of the Liaohsi-Shenyang campaign, see *Peking Review*, no. 46 (November 17, 1972), pp. 12–16. Also see *New York Times*, December 17, 1972.

in what China does. Although it is very difficult to obtain reliable information, there are five insurgencies in south-east Asia (omitting the special case of Indochina) that were in varying stages of development at the end of 1972 and in which China has taken a special interest. These are the ones in Burma, Thailand, Malaysia, the Philippines, and Sarawak.

Ever since 1947 the government of Burma has been threatened by the White Flag faction of the Burmese Communist party. The White Flags differ from the Red Flags (who have today virtually disintegrated) in that they adhere to Chinese concepts of guerrilla struggle and they have long received material and propaganda support from China. However, in 1967 both the violence and the Chinese involvement in this war escalated dramatically as a direct result of the influence of the Chinese Cultural Revolution. In June 1967 Chinese students in Rangoon defied a Burmese government ban on the wearing of Mao badges, which led to violent demonstrations and the deaths of two visiting Chinese technicians. In retaliation Peking denounced the Ne Win government and increased its support for the White Flags. During 1968 heavy fighting erupted in lower Burma between government forces and the insurgents, resulting in the wiping out of the party's forces there. Also during the year, party chairman Thakin Than Tun was assassinated. As a result the insurgency shifted to the northern hills along the Chinese border, where the party set up a "North East Command," and where a Peking-trained Kachin, Naw Seng, took over the leadership. Naw Seng returned to Burma from China during 1968 and brought with him about 300 armed supporters. Ne Win later stated that between January and August of 1969, some 355 insurgents and 133 government troops were killed in heavy fighting in the north. He described the situation as "the most serious threat to the state."

Throughout this period Peking kept the insurgents supplied, offered them sanctuary across the border in China, and glorified their activities in its press. The fighting continued unabated until 1971; and on March 28, 1971, Peking set up a radio station in Yunnan to broadcast to the rebels and people of Burma, the "Voice of the People of Burma," comparable to the "Voice of the People of Thailand" set up in Yunnan in 1962 and the "Voice of the Malayan Revolution" set up in 1969 and broadcasting from Hunan. However, during the same month that the rebel radio started operating, China returned its ambassador to Rangoon, suggesting that Chinese policy toward Burma was beginning to function on two different levels.

During the summer of 1971 General Ne Win visited Peking, where he had a meeting with Mao Tse-tung, and shortly thereafter Sino-Burmese government-to-government relations improved. During 1972, several economic and cultural delegations traveled between the two countries, and China again began supplying economic aid to Burma, which had been suspended since 1967. The insurgency along the northern border continued, however, as did Chinese aid to the rebels and broadcasts over the Voice of the People of Burma in Burmese, Chinese, and the minority languages, Jingpaw and Shan, spoken in the northeast.

Although the most active phases of this insurgency began with the Cultural Revolution and declined as the Cultural Revolution declined, it is not easy to explain why China continued to support the Burmese rebels, thereby preventing the restoration of truly friendly relations with Rangoon. These are some possible reasons: (1) China could not completely halt the insurgency even if it wanted to, since it is ultimately rooted in ethnic strife; (2) China may be trying to preserve its image in the communist world as the champion of armed revolution while attempting to overcome the diplomatic isolation it experienced during the Cultural Revolution; (3) China's hostility to Ne Win may have revived after his 1971 visit, particularly after January 13, 1972, when Burma recognized Bangla Desh, an act interpreted in Peking as pro Soviet and anti Chinese; and (4) China may wish to keep the insurgency alive, despite its supplying of modest amounts of economic aid to Burma, in order to continue sapping the limited resources of the Burmese government, thereby inhibiting any real economic development in Burma and softening it up for a future revolution. China has long sought to promote the arms race between India and Pakistan, since in addition to helping to maintain a balance of power in the subcontinent it also contributes to the ideological proposition that noncommunist regimes in Asia are less effective than China in developing their countries. If a noncommunist state must devote a large part of its budget to counterinsurgency, border patrol, and arms purchases, it has fewer resources to devote to meeting the long-term needs and aspirations of its citizens. It might even fall victim, sooner or later, to a real revolution.[10]

The insurgency in Thailand has a different basis. Daniel D. Lovelace, who has made the most thorough analysis of China's promotion of the Thai insurgency, finds that China generated it in the early sixties in response to the building

[10] On Burma, see Robert A. Holmes, "China-Burma Relations Since the Rift," *Asian Survey* 12, no. 8 (August 1972): 686–700; *Annual of Power and Conflict*, 1971, pp. 50–51; *Current Scene* 10, no. 12 (December 1972): 3–4; and *New York Times*, January 21, 1973.

of American bases in Thailand but that by the end of the decade, as a result of the Cultural Revolution, China was exploiting it primarily to glorify Mao and to attack the Soviet Union.[11] This is surely true, but events after the Cultural Revolution suggest that the insurgency has been redirected toward its original goals. It has not subsided. Throughout the period of China's reemergence on the diplomatic scene, the Thai People's Liberation Armed Forces, made up of Thai villagers, hill tribesmen, and minority nationals, have received propaganda support and training from China. Until the autumn of 1971 most insurgents had been from the Meo tribes in the extreme north and from the Thai-Lao living in the northeast frontier area, but after that communist organizers began, with considerably less success, to try to mobilize lowland villages.

During the spring of 1972 the Royal Thai Army carried out a major counterinsurgency operation at Phu Hin Long Kla plateau in the north, and this widely reported battle seemed to awaken the people of the rest of the country to communist efforts and caused them to rally around the government.[12] By midsummer, for the first time in the history of the Thai insurgency, the government ordered the evacuation of seven entire districts bordering on Laos. Once the inhabitants had been removed, search-and-destroy operations were undertaken. Complicating the picture is a road built by the Chinese from Yunnan province through Houa Khong and Luang Prabang provinces in Laos in the direction of the Thai border. It is expected that this road will

[11] Lovelace, *China and "People's War" in Thailand, 1964–1969* (Berkeley: Center for Chinese Studies, University of California, 1971).

[12] *Far Eastern Economic Review*, March 18, 1972, p. 12. Also see the same journal for June 10, 1972, p. 9; and July 1, 1972, pp. 16, 18.

allow China and North Vietnam to introduce and resupply insurgents in northern Thailand virtually at will.[13]

There have been slight signs of a Chinese shift to a "two-tiered" approach toward Thailand. During 1972 China and Thailand began to exchange sports teams, and there was a gingerly beginning toward informal talks on such problems as the insurgency and the status of the overseas Chinese community in Thailand. The insurgency continues to be confined almost entirely to the northern border areas and has made little headway among the Thai population proper. However, the Chinese are clearly supporting it in conjunction with communist activities in Indochina, and are likely to continue doing so as long as the struggle there goes on.[14]

The Malaysian people's war differs from that of either Burma or Thailand. Following the defeat in 1960 of the Communist party of Malaya's guerrilla war against the British, about five hundred communists took sanctuary across the border in southern Thailand. By 1968 these guerrillas, principally Chinese but with some new recruits from the Malay and Thai communities, had grown to about a thousand, and they reopened guerrilla warfare along the Thai-Malaysia border against the government in Kuala Lumpur. This communist force is reportedly still led by Chin Peng, who headed the guerrillas at the end of the Emergency in 1960.

On November 15, 1969, the Chinese opened a clandestine radio station, the "Voice of the Malayan Revolution," which in its initial broadcast called for an "extensive peo-

[13] Ibid., October 14, 1972, p. 26.

[14] For the outlook in Thailand following the Paris accords of 1973 on Indochina, see the interview with Lt. Gen. Saiyud Kerdpol, director of the Thai Communist Suppression Operations Command, in ibid., March 19, 1973, pp. 26–28.

ple's war" in Malaysia and Singapore. It stated explicitly that the Communist party of Malaya was guided by the thought of Mao Tse-tung. Kuala Lumpur and Bangkok retaliated by setting up a joint antiguerrilla command, and during late 1969 and 1970 these combined forces captured several guerrilla training camps in southern Thailand. In their propaganda the guerrillas have tried to broaden their base of supporters beyond the Chinese by appealing to other ethnic and religious groups, but they seem to have made little progress. The insurgency itself has been confined to terrorist raids, and on May 7, 1970, the Malaysian chief of staff said that he had no evidence of Chinese arms reaching the insurgents.

During May 1971 Tengku Razaleigh Hamzah led a semiofficial trade mission to Peking. In an interview Chou En-lai told him that no big powers should interfere in the affairs of other countries, but on May 19, the New China News Agency (NCNA) wrote, "The Malayan National Liberation Army, under the leadership of the Communist Party of Malaya, has persisted in guerrilla warfare and valiantly struck at the enemy through ambushes, mine warfare and other tactics." The problem in Malaysia is complicated by the fact that the insurgents are mostly Chinese in a nation where ethnicity is the major determinant of all political relationships. China's verbal support for the rebels may reflect an attempt to appeal to the Chinese of southeast Asia more than an effort to promote people's war. In any case, as of 1973 the insurgency was being kept under control by the Malaysian government, and relations between China and Malaysia were slowly unfreezing, although at a much slower rate than Sino-Burmese relations.

In December 1968 in the Philippines, a Maoist faction split off from the Communist party of the Philippines, which is itself further subdivided into two pro-Soviet factions, and a year later this Maoist Communist party created the "New People's Army." Since 1970 the New People's Army has been carrying on widely dispersed guerrilla operations in northeast and central Luzon and winning the enthusiastic endorsement of Peking radio. On October 27, 1970, NCNA identified the chairman of the Maoist party's central committee as Amado Guerrero, an alias of the young, former university professor, Jose Maria Sison. Until he went underground in 1969, he had headed a left-wing student organization in Manila. Sison and other intellectual Maoists have been active in trying to indoctrinate the peasantry, but it appears that at the guerrilla level, the Communist party of the Philippines and the New People's Army rely primarily on former Huks, who today are reportedly free-lance terrorists, formerly communist directed but having lost much of their ideological motivation. During July 1970 President Marcos ordered military operations against the rebels.

On May 19, 1971, NCNA said that the people of the Philippines could take heart from the fact that "the Philippine New People's Army, under the leadership of the Philippine Communist Party, has launched armed struggle vigorously . . . [and] fought more than 80 battles with the reactionary troops and wiped out over 200 enemy men in a little over a year after its founding." Only slight progress has been made thus far in improving relations between Peking and Manila, but during 1972 a growing number of Philippine visitors, including doctors, legislators, and banking and trade groups, traveled to China and were cordially received. China appeared to be interested in developing at least a two-tiered relationship with the Philippines.

Complicating the Philippine picture is another insurgency, unrelated to that of the New People's Army in Lu-zon—namely, the Muslim uprising in Mindanao aimed at secession from the Christian Philippines and union with Muslim Sabah, a part of Malaysia. During 1973 it became clear that Maoists have tried to penetrate the Mindanao movement, but it seemed unlikely that they had met with much success, given the historically religious and nonideo-logical nature of much of the unrest in the southern Philip-pines. The real importance of the secessionist insurgency was its contribution to overall instability throughout the country, thereby draining off valuable resources into coun-terinsurgency and giving the insurgents more propitious circumstances for promoting revolution. President Mar-cos's declaration of martial law on September 22, 1972, re-sulted in an increase of military action against the insur-gents—the government claimed to have killed some 1,757 rebels in the six-month period following martial law—but the Philippine insurgencies and Maoist interest in them persisted with considerable tenacity.[15]

Within the relatively large Chinese community of Sara-wak (i.e., the Eastern Malaysian state located in north Borneo), communism has a long history going back to the Malayan Emergency and to the Indonesian Confron-tation with Malaysia. Communist ideas spread to the ter-ritory through Chinese who visited Singapore, Malaya, and China; and during the early sixties the Sarawak Communist Organization, as it calls itself, opened armed struggle in sup-port of Sukarno's military assault on the new nation of Malaysia. After the abortive 1965 coup in Indonesia, the

[15] See, in particular, Robert Shaplen, "Letter from Manila," *New Yorker*, April 14, 1973, pp. 97–119; "Mindanao: Marcos' Vietnam?" *Far Eastern Economic Review*, March 26, 1973, pp. 13–16; and *New York Times*, December 17, 1972; March 11, 1973; and April 15, 1973.

Chinese communists of Borneo were forced to retreat into Sarawak in order to escape the anti-Chinese pogroms being carried out throughout Indonesia. In the early seventies, under the name of the People's Army of North Kalimantan, about seven hundred communists were still fighting against the federal government, and they received verbal encouragement from Peking (although apparently not arms, judging from the guerrillas' reported dearth of weapons).[16]

On March 25–26, 1972, the Sarawak guerrillas ambushed and killed some fifteen Malaysian Rangers sixty miles west of Kuching. After a visit to the state during the same month by Malaysian prime minister Tun Abdul Razak, the authorities began to carry out a new plan of counterinsurgency—arming the indigenous Iban population with shotguns. Although this move opened up the possibility of the Chinese guerrillas obtaining arms by organizing these peoples, it also held the potentiality of unleashing Iban retaliation against all Chinese. At the end of 1972 the insurgency in Sarawak continued to be very active.[17]

As this record shows, in the years immediately following the Cultural Revolution, China continued to support some people's wars, but it did so at a declining level of intensity and primarily in southeast Asia. As far as is known, China provided material support only in Burma and in countries where the role of the United States had raised major issues of national policy (i.e., Indochina and neighboring countries). China was also active in a propaganda sense in areas where Chinese ethnic minorities formed the hard core of the guerrillas. Given the meager chances of success for any of these insurgencies and the fact that elsewhere in the

[16] *Far Eastern Economic Review*, April 15, 1972, p. 14.

[17] See the useful "Sarawak Case Study" in Douglas Hyde, *The Roots of Guerrilla Warfare* (London: Bodley Head, 1968), pp. 59–128.

Third World China has shifted to a policy of state-to-state cooperation rather than subversion, it is to be expected that China will increasingly deal with its neighboring states in southeast Asia on the basis of the five principles of peaceful coexistence. Needless to say, however, the outcome of the continuing struggle in Indochina, where Sino-Soviet rivalries color all external communist involvement, will greatly influence the pace of this trend.

Finally, in looking back on the decade of the 1960s and China's efforts to turn the grievances of rural Asia into revolution, one cannot fail to record China's dismal performance in the face of the most genuine revolutionary situation of them all—namely, the 1967 Naxalbari peasant uprising in India and its political outcome. The peasants (who also form an ethnic group) of the Naxalbari subdivision of Darjeeling district in the northern portion of West Bengal rebelled and occupied lands in resistance to what they considered unjust and exploitative land tenure conditions. This jacquerie inspired many Maoist intellectuals, dissatisfied with both of the Indian communist parties and their acceptance of parliamentary politics, to organize a third, strictly Maoist party—the Communist party of India (Marxist-Leninist). Although many Indian observers of the new party believed that it was only a terrorist organization and that Chinese-style armed struggle would prove inappropriate in India, events seemed to prove them wrong.

The eruption of the Bangla Desh separatist movement in an area bordering directly on the territory of the "Naxalites" (as the CPI–ML is known) offered ideal conditions for the development of guerrilla warfare. It is doubtful that there existed anywhere else in Asia during the 1960s a more propitious set of circumstances for proving the relevance and validity of Mao's ideas: Bengali desires for economic justice and independence, combined with fierce repression by the troops of West Pakistan, posed conditions not unlike those that prevailed in China at the time of the Japanese invasion.

Unfortunately for the Naxalites, China decided to back West Pakistan in its hopeless campaign of military suppression in Bengal. China's reason, of course, was that the government of India, supported by the Soviet Union, first recognized the plight of the Bengalis and gave them direct military assistance in their war of national liberation. The Sino-Soviet dispute took precedence in Peking over people's war. Some Naxalite leaders backed the Chinese position dutifully, thereby committing political suicide; others tried to stick to the principles of the CPI–ML, although these were now tarnished by Mao's political betrayal, no matter how logical they might have remained in the concrete conditions of Bangla Desh and northeastern India. Thus, ironically, the potentiality for a mass-based guerrilla revolution still exists in India, but should it ever occur it would first have to dissociate itself completely from the Chinese doctrine of people's war.[18]

[18] See, inter alia, Marcus F. Franda, "India's Third Communist Party," *Asian Survey* 9, no. 11 (November 1969): 797–817; K. N. Ramachandran, "Peking and Indian Communism Since 1965," *Current Scene* 8, no. 6 (March 15, 1970): 1–13; Gargi Dutt, "Peking, the Indian Communist Movement, and International Communism, 1962–1970," *Asian Survey* 11, no. 10 (October 1971): 984–991; and *Far Eastern Economic Review*, December 16, 1972, pp. 11–12.

7

Spinoffs from the Doctrine

Chinese communist ideology, like traditional Chinese religion, has tended to divide into "great" and "little" traditions as it has gained adherents around the world. No doubt a connection exists between Mao's fully elaborated theory of people's war and the ideas that come through to a peasant in Africa or a student in Japan who knows nothing more of it than the aphorisms in *Chairman Mao Tse-tung on People's War,* just as there is a relationship between the "Maoist vision" of the Cultural Revolution and the thoughts of the eleven million Red Guards who paraded past the T'ien An Men in 1966 holding up the Little Red Book as a miracle-working amulet. But the connection is often tenuous. Ideology in the mind of one man or a small group of leaders, particularly Marxist-Leninist-Maoist ideology, is rational (if not necessarily reasonable); but for ideology to become more than a way of reasoning or a philosophy, it must inspire people to act. In so doing it appeals to both their minds and their emotions, and in the process ideology often becomes myth.

In addition, ideology is not the property of one man or one party or one country. Having entered the marketplace, a particular ideology may be embraced by many different people, who are of course free to modify it, tinker with it, and violate its internal logic, in light of their own needs, experiences, and even understanding of what they have taken over. This is all by way of saying that the historical Chinese people's war and Mao's generalizations of its particular features into grand theory are undoubtedly the single most important source of precedent for revolutionary theorizing in the contemporary world. However, for the theorists, revolutionaries, and people who came after Mao, the Chinese ideology of people's war is not inviolable. Revolutions other than that of China have contributed to the doctrine of people's war, and many men have modified the doctrine, just as Mao altered some of Lenin's formulas, in order to adapt it to changed international and domestic political conditions. Just as with Vietnamese theories of people's war, these later theories bear a family resemblance to Chinese interpretations of their own experience, but they also differ in critical ways. Such modifications of Mao's theory are no less valid because they are modifications, but it is useful to know what has been modified and to see the consequences of the modifications in practice.

Virtually all post-Maoist theories of people's war divorce guerrilla activities from what Mao would call the "support of the people" and what the Soviets would call a "revolutionary situation." They are, in fact, addressed to the problem that mass support for a revolutionary cause does *not* exist; and they attempt to answer the question "What is to be done?" (other than merely waiting) in light of that situation. Theories that advocate guerrilla activity in lieu of a popular infrastructure are designed to elicit one of three kinds of "intervention": intervention by foreign imperialist forces, whose depredations may bring about the mobilization of the masses (e.g., the Japanese in China or the Americans in Vietnam); intervention by international socialist forces in order to support a struggling revolutionary party and to prevent reactionaries from gaining power by defeating the guerrillas (e.g., the Soviets in Cuba or the Indians in Bangla Desh); and intervention by the masses of a country themselves as their aspirations for dignity and social change are mobilized by the examples of heroism that the guerrillas provide.

Based on the Cuban experience and an analysis of what he believed to be the political realities of Latin America, Guevara's theory of guerrilla warfare is intended to elicit the first and third types of intervention. Interestingly enough, the Chinese never mention Guevara in their publications, while the Soviets attack him indirectly, through Régis Debray, who tried to schematize some of his ideas. Guevara himself summarized his theory as follows: "We consider that the Cuban revolution contributed three fundamental lessons to the conduct of revolutionary movements in America. They are: (1) popular forces can win a war against the army; (2) it is not necessary to wait until all conditions for making revolution exist; the insurrection can create them; and (3) in underdeveloped America the countryside is the basic area for armed fighting."[1]

Debray developed these ideas further in his theory of the *foco insurreccional*, or nucleus of armed men, who themselves attempt to create a revolutionary situation by making armed attacks on police and government officials. At the outset, when the guerrillas are spreading the chaos that they hope will lead to mobilization, they do not want involve-

[1] Che Guevara, *Guerrilla Warfare* (New York: Monthly Review Press, 1961), p. 15.

ment by the peasantry, who at this stage will mistrust the guerrillas and may betray them.[2] Debray's essential ideas are contained in these statements from his *Revolution in the Revolution:*

> The guerrilla force is the party in embryo. This is the staggering novelty introduced by the Cuban revolution.
> Any guerrilla movement in Latin America that wishes to pursue the people's war to the end . . . must become the unchallenged political vanguard.
> The people's army will be the nucleus of the party, not vice versa. The guerrilla force is the political vanguard *in nuce* and from its development a real party can arise.[3]

Needless to say, this approach did not work when it was implemented in Bolivia in the sixties. Huntington offers this explanation of its failure:

> The 1960s saw the emergence of a new doctrine of revolutionary war which, perhaps more than anything else, played a role in leading to the defeat of revolutionary movements. This doctrine, reflected in the writings of Che and Debray, marked a major Latin American deviation from the classic Asian doctrine of revolutionary warfare as it had been developed by Mao, Ho, and Giap. The new doctrine put the emphasis on the importance of subjective factors of will and dedication as against objective social conditions. It stressed the role of the guerrilla *foco* itself as against the Maoist stress on the need for popular support. It exalted military factors over political ones, including the significance of the guerrilla force as compared to the party organization. It also, at least in Guevara's formulation, put an emphasis on a continental appeal as against nationalist appeals in in-

[2] Jack Woddis, *New Theories of Revolution, A Commentary on the Views of Frantz Fanon, Régis Debray, and Herbert Marcuse* (London: Lawrence and Wishart, 1972), p. 261.

[3] R. Debray, *Revolution in the Revolution* (New York: Grove Press, 1967), pp. 106, 109, 116.

dividual countries. The extent to which doctrine shapes revolution is open to debate in any particular case, but certainly many of the errors which Latin American revolutionaries committed in the 1960s—including those of Che himself in Bolivia—could be explained in terms of the adherence to this militaristic doctrine of insurgency as compared to the earlier Leninist-Maoist emphasis on political action.[4]

Although this analysis is persuasive, it seems to me that the critical element responsible for the collapse of Guevara's activities was the failure to produce intervention of the first type. Had this happened—that is, had the functional equivalent of the Bay of Pigs been elicited in several Latin American countries—it does not seem to me obvious that Guevara would be condemned today for totally misreading the nature and history of people's war. After all, Mao himself in a sense "elicited" the Japanese invasion through the record of his pre-1937 guerrilla activities and by forcing the Kuomintang into an anti-Japanese united front. The Japanese always attempted to justify their intervention in China in terms of the suppression of communism and the anti-imperialist nationalist movement. Guevara's problem was to have acted too precipitously, in the wrong country, and to have forgotten the first rule of all politics: one must survive.

With regard to the third form of intervention, Guevara did attain some degree of success. He did not "vitalize" the rural population, but by his example he did mobilize large numbers of urban, middle-class students throughout Latin America and in industrialized countries elsewhere. Among the successors to Guevara were the urban guerrillas of Bra-

[4] Samuel P. Huntington, "Civil Violence and the Process of Development," International Institute for Strategic Studies, London, *Adelphi Papers*, no. 83 (December 1971), p. 7.

zilian and Uruguayan cities, who for some five years after
Guevara's death in October 1967, captured the headlines of
the world with political kidnappings, airplane hijackings,
robberies, ambushes, assassinations, and urban terrorism.
Although, as Robert Moss argues, it is difficult to find an
explicit theoretical rationale for such activities among the
groups themselves, it seems to me that the implicit rationale can be found in a look at their attitudes toward
intervention.[5]

So far, Latin American urban guerrillas have not seriously
attempted to elicit external imperialist intervention (although they have kidnapped American diplomatic representatives); and one of the reasons for the shift to the cities
after Guevara's death was because support of the second
type—from Cuba and other local communist parties—was
dwindling for rural revolt. The guerrillas do, however, continue to believe that by their very example they can attract
the population to the support of the revolution and expose
to the people the alleged corruption and brutality of the
ruling establishment. If there is any one thing that urban
guerrillas seek to acquire through their activities, it is pub-
licity; as Carlos Marighella once pointed out, the money
that he and his companions made in a 1968 robbery of a
payroll van ($9,500) was nothing compared to the value of
the coverage the robbery got in the mass media (estimated
at around $400,000 if paid for in the form of advertise-
ments).[6] Unfortunately for the guerrillas, the arousal of the

[5] Robert Moss, "Urban Guerrillas in Uruguay," *Problems of Communism* 20, no. 5 (September–October 1971): 14–23. On the back-
ground causes of urban guerrilla warfare in Uruguay, see M. H. J.
Finch, "Three Perspectives on the Crisis in Uruguay," *Journal of Latin
American Studies* 3, no. 2 (1972): 173–190.

[6] In Moss, *Problems of Communism*, pp. 14–15. Another reason
for the guerrillas' shift to the cities was, of course, the changing de-

masses by "propaganda of the deed" usually fails for the simple reason that, as Huntington puts it, "the criminalization of political violence is more prevalent than the politicization of criminal violence."[7] As in the case of the Tupamaros, the public comes to see their criminal acts as criminal, not political, and when that happens the continuation of the guerrilla movement loses any further rationale.

Despite the failure of most urban guerrilla activities, the point should not be missed that they aim at the mobilization of the masses, either by eliciting the first or second forms of intervention or by mobilizing the masses directly through capturing their attention and inspiring them. In this sense such activities are a form of incipient people's war; the very essence of all theories of guerrilla warfare is to create a popular infrastructure that will provide the military activists with an intelligence advantage against their professionalized adversaries. In authentic revolutionary situations the masses themselves are already mobilized and are seeking leaders. In derivative revolutionary situations, such as those under discussion here, self-proclaimed leaders are trying to stir up the masses. Intervention of various kinds can accomplish the mobilization of the people, but

---

mography of Latin America; over 50 percent of the populations of Uruguay, Chile, Argentina, and Brazil lives in cities.

[7] Huntington, "Civil Violence," p. 15. Of course, the politicization of criminal violence does sometimes occur. "The motives behind terrorism," write Segre and Adler, "vary and are not always discernable; and the borderlines between banditry and terrorism are not clear-cut since motives tend to shift. Recall the classic examples. Pirates could achieve respectability and join the legitimate establishment by being commissioned as privateers. Some, like Sir Henry Morgan, alternated between privateering and buccaneering at their convenience. The Mafia started out as a national liberation movement and eventually organized international crime." "The Ecology of Terrorism," *Encounter* 40, no. 2 (February 1973): 20.

as the case of contemporary Ulster seems to indicate, even when the armed activities of the urban guerrillas have elicited all three kinds of intervention—by the British army, by socialist and ethnic allies with arms and propaganda, and by the masses themselves, who have been forced to pay attention to the guerrillas' cause—the people may still hold the guerrillas responsible for these disturbances, and the revolution will fail.

Intervention of the first two types refers, of course, to direct intervention by outside parties into the internal affairs of another country. The third form of "intervention" is different: it refers to the mobilization of the people either by inspiring them to action or as a result of drastic changes in their political environment. According to the theories of some urban guerrillas, this later condition can be achieved by eliciting through terrorism and outrages a counterinsurgent overreaction from the authorities, one that so disorients the people—who are actually innocent bystanders—that they become covertly engaged on the side of the rebels. As was mentioned in chapter 3, however, terrorism most commonly inspires a military coup d'etat, which may indeed disorient all of the people but which rarely produces a "revolutionary situation" in the Leninist sense. One would have supposed that this lesson had been learned once and for all in 1933, when the policies of the German Communist party helped to elicit Hitlerism and a very different kind of revolution than had been predicted by the German communists.

What urban guerrillas actually hope to generate is a blundering and inept counterinsurgent reaction—something similar to President Ngo Dinh Diem's response to the Buddhist protests in South Vietnam in 1963. The case of

Northern Ireland is ambiguous precisely because the response, particularly at the political level, has itself been ambiguous: terrorism by the Irish Republican Army elicited a hardening of Protestant positions and a consequent partial mobilization of the Catholic population, but it also caused British intervention, in the interests of a just solution and an end to terrorism by both sides. Actually, and contrary to Herbert Marcuse's views (quoted in chapter 3), a successful counterinsurgency is more easily accomplished against urban guerrillas than against rural guerrillas, particularly if external intervention is only a remote possibility and the population, even if somewhat critical of its own government, perceives the behavior of the revolutionaries as criminal.

Japan offers an example. On October 21, 1969, the superintendent of the Tokyo Metropolitan Police, Akira Hatano, announced:

> According to our composite information, guerrilla warfare is likely to occur in many different sections of the city. Radical students who believe in "violent revolution" will attack according to plan using Molotov cocktails. . . . There is simply no logical basis for violent revolution in an advanced industrial nation. Although we do not deny the students the right to protest against the present system, we must deny them their use of violence. . . . I believe that in the near future the students will realize that they are pursuing an erroneous strategy.[8]

[8] The quotation and following information on the Kidōtai is from Ishitani Tatsunari, *Kidōtai to seishun* (The Mobile Forces and Youth) (Tokyo: Ēru Shuppansha, 1970), pp. 10–11 and passim. The translation from the Japanese is by the author. Also see Ebashi Wataru, "Nanajū nendai shakai to chian taisei" (The Society of the Seventies and the System for Maintaining Public Peace and Order), *Hōritsu jihō* (Law Review), special edition on "Maintaining Order and Human Rights," June 1970, pp. 199–204.

Hatano's answer to the students was to use the famed Tokyo Kidōtai, or "mobile forces." Equipped with high-pres-
sure water cannon, barricade-destroying vehicles, search-
light trucks, armored personnel carriers specially designed
for use in cities, and a vast array of other material, and employing tactics that sound like Mao's—that is, concentrate
one's forces for any battle, occupy a better position than the
enemy's, attack when the enemy has begun to falter—the
Kidōtai is probably the most effective counterinsurgent
force operating in an advanced democracy. Standing behind it is an elaborate police intelligence service, including
the capacity to computerize identifying numbers for every
person in Japan if it were necessary, and the Japanese Self-
Defense Forces, with whom the police have trained, in case
the police are overwhelmed.[9]

In a large public opinion poll of attitudes toward the use
of the Kidōtai at Tokyo University on January 18 and 19,
1969, some 77 percent backed the police actions. On the
question of the ferocity of the police, 30 percent thought
that they should be more severe, 38 percent thought that
they were about right, and 8 percent thought that they were
excessively forceful (the remaining 24 percent had no opinion one way or another). In this respect, it should be noted
that the Kidōtai does not use lethal force. However, even in
cases where the public actively supports the revolutionaries
and where there is no suggestion of criminality in the use of
revolutionary violence, the urban environment offers more
possibilities for the success of what Marcuse calls a "final
solution" than does a rural setting—for example, the actions of the Soviet Red Army in Budapest in 1956.

---

[9] On planning for the use of the Self-Defense Forces and the
Kidōtai against the possibility of an externally fomented insurgency,
see *New York Times,* March 4, 1973.

This is not to conclude that urban guerrilla warfare is a totally hopeless proposition. Perhaps the most important recent case of successful "urban" guerrilla warfare and terrorism was the EOKA (Greek) resistance movement in Cyprus, 1955–1958. There, however, the issue was never one of the guerrillas becoming strong enough to force the withdrawal of Great Britain from the island. It was rather that the Greeks held on long enough to capture international attention, and when that happened they had victory virtually in their hands. The Cypriot insurrection came to involve the foreign relations of three nations—England, Greece, and Turkey—and threatened the whole southern flank of NATO. The essential achievement of EOKA was precisely to bring about this international entanglement, thereby forcing major powers to make choices relatively favorable to its cause. Had the NATO complication not arisen, British counterinsurgent force could have demonstrated to the insurgents the impossibility of success— which is precisely what counterinsurgent *force* is supposed to do.

Urban guerrilla warfare in a modern setting can usually succeed only if it produces a bungled domestic reaction or impinges on international interests in such a way that major powers decide to promote or tolerate a revolutionary "victory" as the better part of a complex bargain. In another recent example, that of the "Che Guevarist" uprising of April 1971 in Ceylon, it appears that the activists hoped to elicit intervention of both the second and third types. It goes beyond the scope of this book to explore the very complex origins of this revolt, but suffice it to say that a large group of educated youths aged sixteen to twenty-five, organized as the "People's Liberation Front," on April 5, 1971, launched a series of armed surprise attacks against almost

seventy-four police stations throughout the country. The
results were an appalling twelve hundred deaths, over US-
$20 million in damages, a doubling of the army and police
manpower in a country that could not afford its preinsur-
gency forces, and between fifteen and sixteen thousand
youths still in jails or rehabilitation camps that could easily
become schools for further revolution.[10] The roots of this
movement are to be found in the unimpressive record of the
government in Ceylon (or Sri Lanka, as it is now called)
since its peaceful achievement of independence in 1948;
but the precipitating factors were youthful dissatisfaction
with the traditional left in Ceylon, the influence of Mao's
and Guevara's ideas about the efficacy and Marxist "correctness" of armed struggle, and the belief (probably erroneous) on the part of the rebels that in their struggle they
could expect foreign assistance from socialist countries, in
particular North Korea and China.[11] The rebels were
avowed followers of both Mao and Guevara, but the appel-
lation "Guevarist" seems to have been attached to them because of their willingness to act without popular backing.
Needless to say, socialist countries did not come to the
Guevarists' support, probably because the government of
Mrs. Sirimavo Bandaranaike against whom they revolted
was (and is) already sufficiently leftist to suit both Moscow
and Peking.[12] The Ceylonese case is interesting in illustrat-

[10] See A. Jeyaratnam Wilson, "Ceylon: A Time of Troubles," *Asian
Survey* 12, no. 2 (February 1972): 109–115; "Politicus," "The April
Revolt in Ceylon," *Asian Survey* 12, no. 3 (March 1972): 259–274;
and *Far Eastern Economic Review*, May 27, 1972, pp. 29–30.

[11] "Politicus," *Asian Survey* (March 1972), p. 272.

[12] For an account of the Guevarist uprising favorable to the rebels
and critical of China's failure to support them, see Fred Halliday,
"The Ceylonese Insurrection," *New Left Review*, no. 69 (September–
October 1971), pp. 55–90. Printed on page 91 is Chou En-lai's mes-

ing a "reverse flow" of revolutionary ideas from Latin America (i.e., Guevaraism) back to Asia. Another example is the Iranian "Tupamaros," a terrorist and guerrilla group inspired by their Uruguayan counterparts and backed by Iraq and by some Arab extremists from the Palestinian movements.[13]

Intervention of the second type—that is, from one or the other socialist bloc countries—does not necessarily mean direct intervention while a revolution is in progress; but the very fact that nations exist that could protect newly installed leftist revolutionary governments from counterrevolution has been a spur to revolutions. Or, at least, so the Soviets think. Pomeroy explains the prevalence of leftists acting in the absence of a revolutionary situation in terms of this factor:

> In the contemporary period the radicalized petty bourgeoisie often seeks to act with impatience, independently and in advance of the proletarian movement, tending to view student and intellectual sectors as the vanguard of the revolution. They seek armed struggle without waiting for a mass upsurge in its varied forms, in the belief that *action* by a minority will create the mass upheaval. No doubt this outlook has been augmented by the growing importance of the external factor in the revolutionary situations of today, by the knowledge that armed strug-

---

sage of April 26, 1971, to Prime Minister Bandaranaike applauding her suppression of the insurrection and stating, "Following Chairman Mao Tse-tung's teaching the Chinese people have all along opposed ultra 'left' and right opportunism in their protracted revolutionary struggles. We are glad to see that thanks to the efforts of Your Excellency and the Ceylon Government, the chaotic situation created by a handful of persons who style themselves 'Guevarists' and into whose ranks foreign spies have sneaked has been brought under control."

[13] *Annual of Power and Conflict*, 1971, Brian Crozier, ed. (London: Institute for the Study of Conflict, 1972), pp. 45–46.

gles can be supported and their victories protected by the socialist and anti-imperialist countries (as in the case of Cuba).[14]

There are no recent cases of revolution-making in the absence of a revolutionary situation which have succeeded in eliciting both the desired form of intervention and the desired effect on the population, but the precedents of people's war and the prevailing international conditions of the sixties and seventies make the attempts plausible.

One further permutation of people's war theory is not based on the attempt to elicit intervention. In the doctrines discussed thus far the problem has been one of how to obtain mass support for the guerrillas; but another, perhaps more basic, problem is how to get guerrillas in the first place, regardless of what the masses are thinking or doing. Lin Piao alluded to the solution to this problem when he spoke of war as a "great school" and of its capacity to "temper" people, but by far the most important writer to address this question is Frantz Fanon. For Fanon the most elementary difficulty in revolution-making is that people who have been socialized in a colonial regime are afflicted with self-doubts, a lack of dignity, and a consequent paralysis of the will to act. He advocates the resort to armed struggle, not in order to obtain some political end but because the use of force tends to transform and liberate some people's personalities. In other words, he favors violence without a revolutionary purpose in order to create revolutionaries. Fanon's position is, of course, a kind of compliment to the influence of French thinking on him: Sorel is well known for his contention that in the violence of political strikes workers could be transformed into "men." Jack

[14] William J. Pomeroy, ed., *Guerrilla Warfare and Marxism* (New York: International Publishers, 1968), p. 39.

Woddis, of the Soviet-inclined British Communist party and a man who is scandalized by Fanon's and Debray's alleged "depoliticization" of revolutionary activity, writes:

> For them [Fanon and Debray] violence is not just a means to an end but a necessary experience in itself; violence is liberation; it is the cleansing fire which tests and purifies revolutionaries. It is, according to Fanon, by practicing violence that the long-subjected colonial peasant overcomes his fear of the enemy and acquires a readiness to take part in revolutionary change. Debray propounds his belief that by the physical act of taking up arms and fighting man transforms himself into a dedicated revolutionary.[15]

Guerrilla warfare as a kind of Third World "encounter group" may sound farfetched, but when it was combined with the impact of the Chinese Cultural Revolution of the late sixties, it began to have an influence on revolutionary activities. Both Fanon and Mao have a profound interest in creating "new men," and both of them think that revolutionary violence, either real or stage-managed as in Mao's Cultural Revolution, is the best way to do so. This idea, when added to the requirement of armed struggle in people's war doctrines, leads directly to such manifestations of contemporary life as university campuses calling themselves "liberated areas"; Milan's millionaire "guerrilla publisher," Giangiacomo Feltrinelli, blowing himself up with dynamite while trying to sabotage a high-tension pylon;[16] and Niiji-

[15] Woddis, *New Theories of Revolution*, p. 398.

[16] For a revealing report on "liberation armies," "red brigades," and numerous armed action groups in Italy, see Claire Sterling, "The Feltrinelli Case," *Atlantic*, July 1972, pp. 11–18. Feltrinelli, whom Sterling calls a "guerrilla publisher," died on March 15, 1972. The publishing house he had inherited published such spectacular successes as *Dr. Zhivago* and *The Leopard*, but Feltrinelli himself was best known as a financial backer for numerous European leftist groups and as an admirer of Che Guevara.

ma's notion that Tokyo students joining together with disgruntled farmers to battle policemen over the government's efforts to build a new Tokyo airport constitutes "people's war" (during September 1971 three policemen were killed in the course of such activities).[17]

This kind of people's war is usually unsuccessful, but it can be and often is justified as being of personal benefit to the participants regardless of its political effects. As J. B. Bell puts it, "The myth of the guerrilla has been extrapolated from a technique of attrition to revolutionary tactics and then to a psychomilitary strategy possessing not only the capacity to win wars of national liberation but also to transform men."[18] The Chinese doctrine of people's war is certainly not responsible for all of these things, nor for the addition to our vocabulary of terms such as "ecology guerrillaism," "guerrilla theater," or "sexual guerrilla warfare"; but it set in motion the thought processes that led, through various byways, to them.

[17] Niijima Atsuyoshi, *Atarashiki kakumei* (New Revolutions) (Tokyo: Keisō Shobō, 1969), pp. 242–243.
[18] *The Myth of the Guerrilla* (New York: Knopf, 1971), p. 59.

8

Conclusion

The people's wars of the 1960s, as sketched in the previous chapters, caused a good deal of mayhem and destruction around the world. Even so, the reader may still ask, are people's wars of any real significance—either as facets of communist societies or as influences on the world balance of power? Numbers of lives lost, as well as pure destructiveness, like natural disasters, are not necessarily adequate criteria of significant political behavior. It could be argued that the Maoist doctrine of people's war was only the ideological tip of a much more complex political iceberg in China and around the world; that people's war was merely the ideological cover for Chinese policies that were actually quite pragmatic and that have largely been abandoned today. In a period in which ideological influences in all countries are allegedly on the wane, doesn't it smack of Cold War disputation and the errors associated with it to single out the ideology of people's war for study? Even though I agree that a purely ideological approach to communist and radical movements is likely to obscure as much as it reveals, and that even the Chinese ideology of people's war can be traced to quite clear bases in Chinese foreign policy objectives, it seems to me that studies such as this point to the continued strength of ideology as an influence on political, and particularly revolutionary, behavior.

No revolution ever occurred without ideology. It is one thing for a citizen to think he knows *why* a revolution is needed; it is quite another to know *how* to go about making a revolution and to know *what* to put in place of the institutions that revolutionary violence destroys. Some people have argued that the revolutionary is like Hercules: having cleaned the Augean stables, he is under no obligation to fill them up again. As a matter of fact, he always does so, obliged or not. Revolutionary ideology supplies answers to the questions why, how, and what—that is to say, it offers a critique of present conditions, a strategy for the use of political violence in order to change those conditions, and a vision of an improved society. It is of course true that leaders and adherents of revolutionary movements are influenced by a variety of motives, and that for an observer to rely solely on an understanding of their shared ideology in trying to explain their behavior would be folly. The problem obviously is not either to ignore or to fixate on the role of ideology in politics but to conceptualize it properly and to study it as one input into the overall processes of political cognition and motivation. In moving away from the Cold War vogue of interpreting all communist behavior in terms of an ideological blueprint, it is nonetheless essential to remember that ideology still influences politics—in communist societies as in all others. The particular forms, the ferocity, and the outcomes of the revolutions of the 1960s are simply unintelligible without reference to the doctrine of people's war and its impact on both the adherents and the opponents of revolution.

If that point is accepted, one might still ask whether people's war as such is, or ought to be, of any interest to peoples not caught up in one. Isn't the real lesson of the 1960s that people's wars were taken far too seriously by countries not afflicted by them, and that, in a sense, if foreigners (and political scientists) would only quit paying attention to them, they would go away—or at least diminish in importance? As Kenneth Waltz argues, "The revolutionary guerrilla wins civil wars, not international ones, and no civil war can change the balance of world power unless it takes place in America or Russia."[1] In this view people's war becomes a non-problem and a non-subject; the real problem is why some people want to meddle in other people's civil wars.

The answer to this line of thinking is rather simple. Regardless of the existential and ideological causes of revolutions, they inevitably boil down to a concern with the enlargement of state power, which is precisely what all successful revolutions of the past two centuries have brought about, notably in China. To quote Ellul, "Whether we like it or not, a type of constant revolution has existed since 1789. Each successful revolution has left the state enlarged, better organized, more potent, and with wider areas of influence; that has been the pattern even when revolution has assaulted and attempted to diminish the state. It is a matter of record which no theory can disprove." For Ellul this relationship between revolution and the growth of the state leads to a definition: "Revolution is finally the crisis of the development of the state."[2] Enlargements of state power inevitably affect the balance of power, and therefore I would argue that "civil wars" in other people's countries are understandably of concern to everybody, or ought to be.

[1] Kenneth N. Waltz, "The Politics of Peace," *International Studies Quarterly* 11, no. 3 (September 1967): 205.
[2] Jacques Ellul, *Autopsy of Revolution* (New York: Knopf, 1971), pp. 160, 162–163.

Waltz is of course correct in arguing that during the period in which a particular society is convulsed by people's war, it can hardly make a contribution to the course of international events, either as an ally or as an enemy. China during World War II illustrates this point perfectly, Allied wartime propaganda notwithstanding. However, as our discussion in the introduction to this essay sought to show, people's wars are not *merely* civil wars; they are also "revolutions." In the modern period revolutions have become the primary subject matter of a global intellectual concern to find patterns of and meaning in history. In our preoccupations with industrialization, modernization, development, and change, revolutions have acquired a "historical significance" that distinguishes them from mere "civil wars" and that transcends specific social grievances and desirable alternatives to present social arrangements. Revolutions *in accordance with one or another theory of history* —and which, when successful, are interpreted as validations of that theory—tend to exaggerate the effect of any particular revolution in the minds both of its adherents and of external observers. If the revolutions in places such as Algeria, Cuba, Egypt, or Vietnam had been conceived of as civil wars, it seems unlikely that the normal enlargement of state power that always follows would have been of concern to any but immediately neighboring countries. However, by adding to these successful revolutions the idea that they were also part of a Rosetta stone to the past and a prophecy of the future, one understands why these cases appeared so important to all politically aware people in the world. Until revolution ceases to be identified with progress in the minds of virtually everybody, no one sensitive to politics is going to treat revolution as if it were merely somebody else's fight.

On the other hand, it is useful to be reminded that

revolutions in the modern sense are also, in fact, civil wars. If other nations want to make a successful adjustment to them, they cannot ignore the fact that a domestic fight is going on between people who are agitated by issues other than the general course of human history. For this reason direct intervention in one is generally the worst thing that a prudent nation can do—not because the revolution is unimportant either ideologically or to the world balance of power but because foreign intervention, if it fails, is bound to antagonize in the most direct manner the victorious revolutionary state. An alternative approach, occasionally available, might be to try to "derevolutionize" a revolution by encouraging the nations of the world to understand it as a civil war. This would at least weaken the ideological multiplier effect: civil wars are not prime concerns of intellectuals and philosophers of history, whereas revolutions are. A Vietnamese "civil war," for example, does not bear the same import as a Vietnamese "revolution." Unfortunately, the Chinese doctrine of people's war made such a separation impossible in Vietnam and in many other places during the 1960s, with consequences that are all too familiar.

All people's wars lay claim to being revolutions, but not all revolutions are people's wars; this distinction suggests that our study of people's war might also offer insights into the vexed problem of why there are *types* of revolutions. The problem itself is obvious: in accordance with the general reductionist approach favored by scholarly analysts of revolution, it is possible to compare many different revolutions on the basis of the structural characteristics of societies and the human grievances that allegedly generate revolutions. However, even though different societies may be quite similar in terms of the roots of revolution, the revolutions themselves take different forms. In some cases the same "causes" produce a military coup d'etat, or a peasant jacquerie, or a political putsch, or a generalized upheaval, or an ethnic civil war, or a communist seizure of power; in others a people's war occurs. Without fully explaining this phenomenon, analysts have tried to bring it under control by constructing "typologies" of revolution. One writer, for example, identifies the following types: palace revolution, communal revolution, co-opted revolution, nationalist revolution, orderly revolution, elite revolution, imposed revolution, and mass revolution.[3] I myself at one time suggested a six-fold typology composed of jacquerie, millennarian revolt, anarchistic revolt, jacobin-communist revolution, conspiratorial coup d'etat, and militarized mass insurrection—a typology that several writers have found of some ad hoc usefulness but have also faulted for its obvious logical deficiencies.[4]

In light of the people's war cases and the continuing proliferation of idiosyncratic typologies, I believe that it is time to take an entirely new tack in approaching this problem. We seem to suffer from too much reductionism and not enough attention to purposive action. It is perfectly sound to try to uncover the socioeconomic roots of behavior—particularly if we wish to change behavior, since these socioeconomic conditions are presumably more amenable to change than are peoples' minds—but in the analysis of behavior it is also necessary to ask directly, what do people engaged in revolution think they are doing? This approach

[3] William Kornhauser, "Revolutions," in Roger W. Little, ed., *Handbook of Military Institutions* (Beverly Hills, Calif.: Sage Publications, 1971), p. 384.

[4] Chalmers Johnson, *Revolution and the Social System* (Stanford: The Hoover Institution on War, Revolution, and Peace, 1964), pp. 26–69. Cf. Lawrence Stone, "Theories of Revolution," *World Politics* 18, no. 2 (January 1966): 162–164; and Perez Zagorin, "Theories of Revolution in Contemporary Historiography," *Political Science Quarterly* 88, no. 1 (March 1973): 50–51.

leads back to the problem of ideology. Although most theorists of revolution recognize the central role of ideology in processes of revolution and often use it as an input in the construction of typologies, their attention has most commonly focused on the critical and goal-identifying functions of ideology. The strategic function has been neglected.

As was stated earlier, revolutionary ideology supplies answers for the potential rebel to the questions of why, how, and what. Many revolutionary situations share common whys and whats; they differ according to hows. Different strategic conceptions of how to bring about change through violence is thus one important source of revolutionary variation. Another source of variation occurs when the whys and whats are radically different but the hows are identical —that is, when strategies that worked in earlier, known revolutions are applied in subsequent revolutions of an entirely different sociological nature and ideological purpose. The instances of people's war seem to belong largely to this latter case.

John Dunn asserts that "revolutions belong to a tradition of historical action in the strong sense that virtually all revolutions in the present century have imitated—or at least set out to imitate as best they could—other revolutions of an earlier date."[5] I should like to supplement this observation with the thought that the revolutions chosen for imitation are not selected randomly. Two additional concepts are needed here, one from the traditions of revolutionary analysis and the other from the logic of scientific conceptualization—namely, the concepts of a "great revolution" and of a "paradigm."

Writers on revolution in the past (e.g., George Pettee and Hannah Arendt) have often restricted the range of

[5] John Dunn, *Modern Revolutions* (Cambridge: Cambridge University Press, 1972), p. 232.

cases considered in their analyses to what they called the "great revolutions," without, however, establishing what it was that made these revolutions great. The cases themselves are obvious: the French, Russian, and Chinese revolutions, occasionally joined by the American revolution and the English revolution of the seventeenth century. I do not dispute that these are the "great" cases, but I should like to suggest that what made them great was the fact that, intellectually, they altered older understandings of the word "revolution" and supplied it with new meaning. They were, in short, paradigmatic cases of revolution, and their influence as paradigms of revolution held sway, wherever revolution was thought about at all, until the next great revolution came along and established a new paradigm. By "paradigm" I mean simply a pattern, example, or model that dominates human thinking to the extent of creating a Gestalt, or an exclusive configuration of thought about a particular subject.[6]

Paradigmatic cases of revolution have supplied answers to other peoples' questions about why to revolt and what to build in place of the targets of revolt, but their primary influence has been in the area of *how* to succeed at revolt. The great revolutions establish the fact that it is possible to revolt and still survive, and they supply procedures for how to go about it. In the wake of all great revolutions the victorious revolutionaries themselves write up paradigm-creating versions of how they did it—Lenin's *"Left-Wing" Communism* and Lin Piao's *Long Live the Victory of People's War!* are examples—and they disseminate these materials widely. One aspect of a great revolution is its active propagation for about a generation at least of its own ideology, sometimes because such missionary activity is called for by

[6] Cf. Thomas S. Kuhn, *The Structure of Scientific Revolutions* (Chicago: University of Chicago Press, 1962).

its ideology, but in any case because evidence of foreign acceptance is useful in legitimizing the new revolutionary regime.

In addition, domestic and foreign writers further spread the message that a genuine "revolution" has occurred by writing histories and analyses of it and paeans to it. If there are persons in the world who know why they want to revolt and who believe that a better world is possible but who need to know how to proceed, it is to these official and exegetical writings that they will turn.[7] In the nineteenth century they read about the French revolution; in the interwar period of the twentieth century they read about the Bolshevik revolution; and since 1949 they have been reading about the Chinese revolution. There has been, in short, a progression in revolution-making from what might be called the Parisian paradigm, to the Comintern paradigm, to the guerrilla paradigm.

Needless to add, the prevailing paradigm will influence others besides active revolutionaries, and it will define normal connotations of the concept of revolution in all ordinary discourse. In one period the term will evoke visions of the Bastille, the guillotine, and barricades; in another, of workers' organizations, "socialism in one country," and Stalinism.[8] Progressive people and sympathizers with the revolution will adopt the styles and modes of thought captured by the paradigm (that we are currently living in the age of the guerrilla paradigm can be confirmed by a visit to any American college campus and observing the costumes

---

[7] For a vivid illustration of committed revolutionaries in the act of searching the known cases for an effective strategy, see Sheridan Johns, "Obstacles to Guerrilla Warfare—A South African Case Study," *Journal of Modern African Studies* 11, no. 2 (1973): 14–18.

[8] In order to observe the changes in symbols of revolution over time, see David Caute's heavily illustrated book *The Left in Europe Since 1789* (New York: McGraw-Hill World University Library, 1966). Needless to add, during the Comintern paradigm even the

of the students). To talk about revolution in ways different from that of the paradigm still requires that homage be paid to the paradigm if one wishes to communicate and be understood—hence such neologisms as "urban guerrilla warfare," "Third World people" (for Americans of non-European ancestry), and "liberation fronts" of all kinds.

"Paradigms" must be carefully distinguished from their "paradigmatic cases," for the two are never identical. Paradigms are constructed by victorious revolutionaries and other observers on the basis of the paradigmatic case in accordance with what they believe, want to believe, or want others to believe really happened. But a revolutionary paradigm is not a history, and, in general, a person who wanted to read a history of a paradigmatic case would be seriously misled if he chose instead to read the materials of the paradigm (Lenin and Lin Piao, for example, say almost nothing about the effects of the two world wars in paving the way for their revolutionary victories). To take a recent example, Guevara explicitly conceived of his writing on guerrilla warfare as a summation of the lessons of the Cuban revolution. However, he omitted to mention that in the anti-Batista struggle he and Castro led a broadly based front of moderates as well as radicals and that Castro was not identified as a communist revolutionary dictator until well after he had come to power. "Bourgeois forces in Cuba and in the United States," writes Davis, "were confused as to where their interests lay during the anti-Batista struggle. The later insurgencies, in contrast, were self-defined as rad-

---

opponents of the Left worked within the prevailing paradigm. Nolte, for example, defines fascism as "anti-Marxism which seeks to destroy the enemy by the evolvement of a radically opposed and yet related ideology and by the use of almost identical and yet typically modified methods, always, however, within the unyielding framework of national self-assertion and autonomy." Ernst Nolte, *Three Faces of Fascism* (New York: Holt, Rinehart, and Winston, 1966), pp. 20–21 and passim.

ical and revolutionary from the start. Moderate and con-
servative forces, especially the ruling elements at home,
were forewarned. Thus the [Guevarist] insurgencies in their
formative stages had little chance either of being ignored or
tolerated as unimportant by the government, or of gaining
broad support from politically-active groups."[9] Guevara
was unable to replicate the Cuban revolution in other Latin
American countries in part because his paradigm of the
Cuban revolution did not square with the paradigmatic
case. This distinction between paradigm and case—between, for example, Lin Piao's tract and the actual history
of China between 1937 and 1949—goes a long way toward
explaining why the Chinese-sponsored people's wars of the
1960s met with so little success.

The existence of paradigms of revolution contributes to
the variation in form and outcome of revolutionary attempts over time and space, but no suggestion is intended
that all revolutions of a particular period conform to identical strategies. Paradigms do not work that way; they
merely establish the prototypes from which many variations
will be developed. Mao was experimenting within the Leninist paradigm for many years before he perfected his own
strategy. Over time and as the cases build up testifying to
the failure of the paradigm in differing circumstances, new
methods will be tried. If and when a new great revolution
occurs, it will sweep away the influence of the old paradigm.
In the interim new paradigms will be proposed, often oriented toward overcoming the failures of the prevailing paradigm, but until a paradigmatic case validates them once
and for all, they will remain experimental. For example,
German radicals today have come up with a revolutionary

[9] Jack Davis, "Political Violence in Latin America," International
Institute for Strategic Studies, London, *Adelphi Papers*, no. 85 (February 1972), pp. 13–14.

strategy they call *Systemüberwindung* (conquest of the system) and which has been described as follows: "The common element of this strategy lies in the perversion into weapons of the fundamental moral and political values which underlie these institutions [i.e., "institutions which rest on opinion rather than on force"]; the aim is to undermine their stability by the use of their own values and beliefs."[10] Although this judo-like playing on the target system's values has had some success in Germany and has affinities with the North Vietnamese "externalization program," this German strategy remains untested. The world has not yet come to regard the Berkeley-Paris-Tokyo radical student syndrome as either a great revolution or a paradigmatic case.

In sum, "people's war" originated as a distillation of the experiences of the Chinese communists in the Chinese revolution. The fact that the communists have tried to propagate their doctrines in areas outside of China is in no way unusual. Every great revolution, most particularly the American, French, and Russian revolutions, gave rise to the same kind of political activity. If, in fact, the evidence proves accurate that the Chinese are now ending their period of active revolutionary ecumenicism, then we must conclude that the Chinese revolution generated no longer nor more destructive a period of such activity than the American revolution did in Latin America, the French revolution in western Europe, or the Russian revolution in eastern Europe. This is, of course, no consolation for the peoples who have happened to be in the paths of any of these great revolutions.

[10] Helmut Schelsky, "The Strategy of 'The Conquest of the System': The Long March Through the Institutions; The Wider Setting of Disorder in the German Universities," *Minerva* 10, no. 4 (October 1972): 616.

Index